£10

HIGHWAYMEN
AND
OUTLAWS

Jesse James. (Library of Congress, LC-USZ62-3855)

MICHAEL BILLETT

HIGHWAYMEN

AND

OUTLAWS

ARMS AND
ARMOUR

Dedicated to the memory of my daughter
Jenny

Arms and Armour Press
An Imprint of the Cassell Group
Wellington House, 125 Strand, London WC2R 0BB

Distributed in the USA by Sterling Publishing Co.
Inc., 387 Park Avenue South, New York, NY
10016-8810.

British Library Cataloguing-in-Publication Data:
a catalogue record for this book is available from
the British Library

ISBN 1-85409-318-5

Designed and edited by DAG Publications Ltd.
Designed by David Gibbons; layout by Anthony A.
Evans; edited by John Gilbert; printed and bound
in Great Britain.

Acknowledgements
A wide variety of sources was consulted in the
preparation of this volume. In particular, I would
like to acknowledge and thank the following
individuals and organisations who assisted with
information and illustrations: Philip Haythorn-
thwaite, Tim Kitchin, Fred Wilkinson, Bank of
England Museum (London), Bibliothèque Nationale
de France (Paris), British Sporting Art Trust
(Newmarket, England), Guildhall Library
(London), Library of Congress (Washington, DC),
Local History Department of Wandsworth Library
(London), National Archives and Records
Administration (Maryland, USA), State Library of
New South Wales (Sydney) and Yorkshire County
Library (York).

CONTENTS

An armed bushranger prepares to mount and join his waiting companions.
(State Library of New South Wales)

INTRODUCTION

The words highwayman and outlaw evoke in many minds the image of a masked, mysterious rider on horseback who robbed the rich and sometimes even gave to the poor. The English highwayman, in particular, was often seen as a dashing, carefree and exciting land pirate on horseback, certainly displaying more gallantry than the lowly criminal who slyly picked pockets or locks. The bold rider was assumed to show no trace of fear when face-to-face with the hapless traveller whom he waylaid. In legend, the English highwayman or 'tobyman', showed chivalry towards the fair sex and by doing so gained many admirers in their midst.

Several English highwaymen were fallen aristocrats, which made them even more fascinating to the public. Unfortunately, such cavaliers, or 'gentlemen of the road', who politely raised their hats before barking 'stand and deliver', were rare. In reality, the vast majority of highwaymen and outlaws were uncouth and foul-mouthed. They included ruthless criminals, like Dick Turpin, who robbed purely for gain. Several were also murderers who showed little compassion towards their victims, especially if they thought they would be recognised later.

The term 'outlaw' had fewer romantic connotations. Originally, any man declared an outlaw could be hunted with impunity and even killed, as he was not entitled to legal protection. Later, the term came to mean any fugitive from the law.

In America, the legend of the Wild West frontier outlaw fighting a fair duel in a fast gun-draw confrontation with a sheriff or marshal was in most cases untrue. Evidence shows that notable gunfighters such as the outlaw Jesse James, Sheriff Pat Garrett, Marshal 'Wild Bill' Hickok and Texas outlaw John Wesley Hardin, were all killed by shots in the back. The most famous outlaw of the Southwest, 'Billy The Kid', was shot by Sheriff Garrett when caught by surprise in a dimly lit bedroom. Wyatt Earp's brother Morgan was shot in the back as he played billiards in a saloon.

In America, the term 'road agent' was often used to describe the outlaw who robbed lone travellers and stage-coaches. The Australians knew him as a 'bushranger'.

During the seventeenth and eighteenth centuries, prior to the age of railways, the English highwayman roamed the roads, robbing individual travellers, stage-coaches and mail-coaches. By the time the railways became established in England in the middle of the nineteenth century, the menace of the highwayman had been virtually eliminated, due mainly to better policing.

In Australia, too, when railways arrived in the later decades of the nineteenth century, only the infamous Ned Kelly gang was still operating. During the earlier part of that century, however, Australian bushrangers had the additional option of ambushing gold shipments being transported by horse, particularly in Victoria and then, to a lesser extent, in New South Wales, Queensland and Western Australia. They also later robbed banks.

These additional options also applied to the American Western outlaw during the various gold strike periods in California, Idaho and Montana. With the coming of the railways, he could further diversify, as did Jesse James, into robbing trains, and subsequently to holding up banks when they became more widely established.

One common factor, nevertheless, applied to the English highwayman, the American Western outlaw and the Australian bushranger; most of them died young and violently, seldom living beyond the age of thirty. Those who lived by the gun died by it, or by the hangman's noose. The few who survived the ultimate penalty endured long prison sentences or, in the case of English highwaymen, transportation to the colonies in America and later Australia; but fewer still were the successful highwaymen and outlaws who were never caught by the forces of law.

England was perhaps unique in having several famous highwaywomen, some of whose exploits were as notorious and daring as those of their male counterparts. England was also exceptional in expecting its highwaymen to behave with dignity and an air of bravado at their own executions, especially those held at Tyburn in London. Many entertained the huge crowds at the gallows with farewell speeches, often mocking the attendant officers of the law.

Although the English highwayman sometimes killed his victim, he was certainly less likely to do so than his European counterpart. No official crime statistics were kept in England before 1805, but study of eighteenth-century court records shows that the murder rate in England was the lowest in Europe, despite the fact that at the same time it possessed the highest robbery rate.

More common in Europe than the individual highwayman or the small gangs prevalent in England, America and Australia, were the many large bandit bands which operated through many centuries, especially in Italy, France and Spain. Although criminal in activity, many bandit lords claimed they were acting politically to achieve justice from the legal but oppressive régime that governed them. Once they were captured, the authorities showed little or no mercy. The bandit leaders were frequently hanged or suffered a painful and lingering death by being broken-at-the-wheel.

A brigand in Northern India, at the end of the eighteenth century, seizing a minister's children as hostages.

The vast majority of the populace, living in abject poverty and misery, supported the bandits against the law enforcers. The bandits, in turn, sometimes gave a little of the money they had stolen from the rich to the sympathetic poor, but seldom out of charity, rather to ensure that they were unlikely to be betrayed to the authorities. Most poor peasants admired the bandits as courageous symbols of protest, social revolt and revenge against their harsh landlords and governments. As a consequence, they built up a wealth of folklore about the bandits and their leaders, in a similar way to the English with their legendary Robin Hood and, later, the Australians with their own folk-hero, Ned Kelly and the Americans with 'Billy The Kid'.

Large bandit bands also roamed in many other countries, including India and Mexico. The dacoits or brigands of India, for example, at times controlled significant areas of territory. When the British brought the railways to India in the latter part of the nineteenth century, the dacoits diversified and reduced their violent sorties on horse and foot, instead travelling on the trains to rob the passengers. In 1887, it was estimated that over 9000 dacoits were still operating in India; in addition to their many robberies, they were responsible for numerous murders.

In Mexico, some of the many bandit bands claimed to be revolutionaries, engaging in guerrilla warfare as well as robbery. The Mexican brigand Cortina made many raids into Texas before the American Civil War. At the end of the nineteenth century, Pancho Villa, perhaps the most famous revolutionary and outlaw in Mexico, led several revolts against successive Mexican governments. He controlled a very large bandit army in the north of Mexico and, like Cortina before him, undertook many raiding incursions into Texas. Eventually, he disbanded his outlaw army, after reaching an agreement with the Mexican government. Later, he was assassinated.

In many countries the highwayman, the outlaw and the bandit band thrived because of weak government, poor administration and lack of adequate policing, especially in rural areas and the early frontier lands. Their numbers invariably grew when wars ended, freeing many already hardened criminals and forcing other ex-soldiers, because of economic circumstances, to pursue a life of crime. In England, the formation of the Bow Street Runners brought a dramatic decline in the many highway robberies which plagued the fringes of London. In America, a mixture of vigilantes, sheriffs, Federal Marshals, Pinkerton detectives and Texas Rangers greatly curtailed the activities of the Western out-

law. In Mexico, the 'Rurales' mounted police and militia caused the demise of the bandit bands. Similar combinations of police and militias, eventually supported by the public, gradually helped to control the outlaws in most other countries.

The following pages concentrate more on the colourful and often brutal characters, sometimes cold-blooded killers, who took to horseback in the nineteenth century, rather than the so-called politically motivated bandits. Mounted highwaymen, of course, have long been replaced in our time by a new breed of villain, using modern, faster forms of transport, and more lethal weapons. But in essence the present is no different from the past. As this book aims to show, the harsh reality of highway crime through the centuries tells a story that, for all its enticing trappings, quite contradicts the legends, myths, romantic fables, poems and latter day fictional film images of highwaymen and outlaws.

Gen. Pancho Villa, Mexican bandit. 1. Gen. Fierro. 2. Gen. Villa. 3. Gen. Ortega.
4. Col. Medina. c. 1913. (National Archives, Maryland, USA)

CHAPTER ONE

HIDE-OUTS AND DISGUISES

Highwaymen and outlaws generally operated on main routes, rather than minor ones, because these were most regularly frequented by travellers, stage-coaches, mail-coaches and gold shipments. Less adventurous bandits were also attracted to the isolated farm or lonely village. A few of the bolder ones went so far as to hold up their victims in broad daylight in the heart of cities, such as London. But wherever he roamed, in order to survive, the highwayman needed a safe refuge to which to retire after completing his robbery. Any remote countryside of woods, hills or mountains and wild rough terrain offered security, as did a large town or city where he could disappear among the crowded streets to a safe lodging. London, for example, additionally offered the advantage of providing 'fences' to whom he could readily dispose of loot.

A crowded English coaching scene - highwaymen loitered at departure points to select potential victims to rob later on the road. Painting by Charles Cooper Henderson. c. 1830. (British Sporting Art Trust)

HIDE-OUTS

Several English highwaymen found secure shelter in the coaching inns of the time. Many of the proprietors and landlords protected them from the law, as frequently they worked in partnership with them and shared the booty. Failing this, the compliant landlords would be handsomely rewarded. Thus the crowded throngs in coaching inn yards often concealed highwaymen on the look-out for potential victims, once their coach had departed a few miles into the night. Many different inns were used for the nocturnal sorties of highwaymen, as, for example, the White Swan in Whitechapel, the Saracen's Head in Aldgate, the Spaniards on Hampstead Heath, the Green Man on Putney Heath, the George at Woolwich and the Old Magpie on the Bath Road. Most were located on the fringes of London, convenient launching pads for holding up coaches.

The majority of seventeenth- and eighteenth-century highwaymen tended to favour concealment in a city, town or coaching inn. Dick Turpin, however, had a hide-out in Epping Forest, and some of his predecessors built themselves crude huts near Waltham Cross. Likewise, in the early thirteenth century, the legendary Robin Hood, according to ballads written about him and his 'merry men', found shelter and safety in Sherwood Forest in Nottinghamshire, just as the early outlaws in Scotland sought refuge in the wilds of the Highlands.

A few American outlaws had impregnable lairs in the mountains, such as the 'Hole-in-the-Wall' gang at the end of the nineteenth century in Wyoming, as also did many of the earlier Spanish, Italian and Mexican bandits. The mountainous retreats gave the outlaws the opportunity to defend themselves, in the event of their being tracked by police or military. Some also relied on the tacit support given by the poor of nearby villages or towns, who warned them of the approach of the law. If these hide-outs were near a trade route, then the combination formed classic bandit territory. Also, any road passing through dense thicket, wilderness and dark swampland was ideal for crime.

The vast, wild, uninhabited and hostile bush of Australia provided a safe hiding-place for the bushrangers because it was virtually inaccessible to the forces of law and order. In the early days, the bushrangers found shelter there in remote huts or caves. In the second half of the nineteenth

The vast deserted Australian bush offered bushrangers both safe hiding-places and ambush points. (Author's Collection)

An English flintlock man-stopper pistol, c. 1800, with a large bore barrel firing a large-sized ball. The muzzle-loading pistol could be fitted in the pocket and was an ideal weapon for travellers to carry, in case of ambush. (Courtesy of Sotheby's)

century, they gained some sympathy from many of the country people, who in return offered them refuge and sometimes even entered into league with them.

Until the mid-nineteenth century, many outlaws throughout the world operated in frontier regions, enabling them, when pursued too closely by the forces of law in one state, to flee for safety across the border into another. This was no longer an option when frontiers were more strongly guarded, co-operation on both sides increased, and pursuit across state borders sometimes authorised.

AMBUSH PLACES

In early Georgian times, historians reported the roads in England to be a disgrace, hardly more than rutted mud tracks. Little road building had been done since Roman times, except for some limited work carried out by the monasteries to allow pilgrims to travel more easily along estab-

lished routes. When Henry VIII closed the monasteries, the situation deteriorated further. This triggered the first Highway Act of 1555 which made each parish responsible for the upkeep of its roads. As most parishes were poor, little improvement was evident, especially as local labourers had compulsorily to spend six days a year repairing the roads. The work known as 'Statute Labour' was unpaid and hence highly unpopular.

Later, in 1654, road rates were introduced which allowed surveyors to pay for the necessary labour. Apparently this marginally improved roads but the resulting increase of wheeled vehicles negated this advance, especially in areas where clay soils predominated. As a result, steps were taken to try to reduce the traffic volume of horse-drawn wagons and carts. Various Acts of Parliament were passed to encourage the use of broad-wheeled conveyances in the hope that the wider wheels would roll the rutted surfaces flat.

A deserted English common – highwaymen favoured such places to waylay their victims.
(Author's Collection)

In practice, however, the reverse occurred and the road surfaces were churned up into a thick muddy clay consistency, with even larger ruts when dry weather came to harden them.

The bad condition of the roads, up to the early nineteenth century, greatly assisted the highwayman in his work. It slowed down the carriages and coaches on long-distance travel to no more than an average of four miles per hour, making the task of interception and robbery much easier. Frequent breakdowns with broken wheels and axles also rendered the stranded vehicle an even easier target for the highwayman. The state of the roads, a scanty police force and the invention of the flintlock pistol, as an alternative to the use of the sword and the earlier unreliable pistols, contributed notably to the success of the English highwayman during the late seventeenth and eighteenth centuries. Moreover, the population in England in the seventeenth century was a sparse six million and there were large expanses of deserted forests and unenclosed heathlands which left travellers inviting targets for attack.

Highwaymen particularly favoured as ambush places the roads running uphill, which slowed down travellers. Gad's Hill, near Rochester on the London Road, for example, was traditionally an especially dangerous and notorious spot. Many famous people were robbed there, including ambassadors, dukes and many seafarers journeying to London from the coastal ports. Because of its reputation, Shakespeare even featured it as the location for the robbery of Sir John Falstaff in *Henry IV*.

Many other hills close to London, such as Shooter's Hill on the London to Dover Road and Highgate Hill in north London were nearly as dangerous. The Bull Inn, on Shooter's Hill was the first posthouse from London where the horses were changed. It therefore attracted highwaymen who gathered there to select potential victims. Ironically, many of these highwaymen also met their doom there, as a gallows was

A tree-lined route through an English wood – an ideal ambush location for a highwayman. (Author's Collection)

erected on the spot. Many were hanged and gibbeted in chains as a grim warning to others. The road from London to Oxford was also dangerous, with highwaymen often lurking in the vicinity of Shotover Hill, near Oxford. In fact, none of the great thoroughfares of the time guaranteed safe travel, one of the very worst being the Great North Road.

Deserted commons and heaths, near cities, were traditional haunts of highwaymen. This especially applied in the eighteenth century when London was undergoing a period of explosive growth, with many more potential victims travelling by horse or carriage. The population of London grew from around 490,000 in 1700 to about 950,000 by 1800. Favourite ambush spots were Hounslow Heath, Putney Heath, Hampstead Heath, Barnes Common, Wimbledon Common and Finchley Common. Hounslow Heath was particularly dangerous because of its thick woodland. Open landscapes, such as Hyde Park to the north and Tothill Fields to the south, were also popular locations to intercept travellers, as was Richmond to the west.

The peril of crossing Finchley Common after dark encouraged many travellers from the north of England to spend the night at Barnet, before undertaking the hazardous journey together in a group the next morning. Similarly, travellers from Bath were reluctant to cross Hounslow Heath in the dark and preferred to stay the night in hostelries at Slough or Colnbrook. In eighteenth-century London, most of the well-known areas now established as parts of the great metropolis were still individual villages surrounded by open countryside. Thus highwaymen still menaced, for example, the approaches to Knightsbridge. Even in the settled areas of central London, during the 1730s, it was not unknown for citizens to be held up in their carriages along the Strand, Cheapside and near St Paul's. Stagecoach robberies were even reported in Soho, Pall Mall, High Holborn and Whitechapel.

No region in the country guaranteed a safe journey from the attention of the highwayman, as travellers across Salisbury Plain and Bagshot Heath often discovered to their cost. The flat open

An unusual thatched former toll-house at Lyme Regis, Dorset, England. Thatch was rarely used on toll-houses because of risk of arson by rioters protesting against tolls. Toll-house keepers warned travellers of highwaymen in the locality but were sometimes robbed themselves. (Author's Collection)

countryside around Newmarket also held dangers to those venturing along the surrounding roads. Not until the end of the eighteenth century did the roads of England afford somewhat safer travel, thanks largely to the institution of a system of turnpike roads and toll-houses. It was one of the duties of the toll-house keepers to warn travellers of highwaymen known to be operating in their area and also to inform the authorities.

Although the establishment of toll-houses and turnpike roads reduced the incidences of highway robbery, passengers faced other new dangers instead. The better roads allowed coaches to travel much faster. Many more accidents occurred because of the increased speed, with collisions, horses bolting and snapped traces all playing a role. It was also not uncommon for drivers to become drowsy and fall asleep, especially after a stop at a coaching inn where they imbibed too freely. Although the horses generally knew the route and kept to the road, they did not always keep to the left-hand side, but tended to gallop on the side that offered the more convenient path for their progress. As a result, a few of the highwaymen who still operated on the turnpike roads may well have been taken by surprise when their intended victim galloped straight past them without heeding their command to stand.

Occasionally there were more isolated hazards. For instance, in 1812 two passengers froze to death when travelling on the mail-coach from London to Bath. In another incident, the passengers travelling on the Exeter to London mail-coach, on the night of 20 October 1816, suffered an even more terrifying experience. A lioness, which had escaped from a travelling menagerie, attacked their coach after they had departed from Salisbury and severely mauled one of the horses before being recaptured. Luckily, while the drama unfolded outside, all but one of the passengers managed to find refuge in a nearby inn, The Pheasant, on Salisbury Plain, where doubtless they quickly fortified their courage with spirits. In their initial panic, however, one unfortunate traveller was locked out of the inn. Although he survived, he never recovered from the shock and was committed to a lunatic asylum for the rest of his life.

The landscape of the American West was, of course, entirely different; and the balance of population changed dramatically when Congress passed the Homestead Act in 1862, offering free land to anyone willing to go out and work it. The vast regions that extended west of the Mississippi to the Rocky Mountains and the prairies and Great Plains were mainly level, open and virtually treeless. In the nineteenth century, during the rapid expansion of the West, and due also to the earlier gold and silver strikes in the Pacific Far West, outlaws were drawn instinctively to the stage-coach and immigrant trails that ran across the open plains. These routes cut through the domains of the native Indians, some of whom were hostile and presented a threat to traveller and outlaw alike. Because of the lack of cover, American outlaws, unlike their English counterparts, often had to chase their victims for many miles before they managed to halt a coach or wagon.

As the railroad pushed farther west in the 1860s, trains carried a wide range of goods and at the railroad halts these were unloaded into wagons for onward transit. Here outlaws gathered to watch and later ambush the wagons; some, like Jesse James, robbed the trains themselves. Small towns with wooden buildings also sprang up alongside the railroads and these, too, were the haunts of bandits. As the rail system expanded, rail ambushes became more frequent, as the raiders resorted to dynamiting the tracks to halt the trains and then using explosives to open the safes in the coaches. During the last decade of the nineteenth century there were 260 train robberies involving the deaths of some ninety passengers and as many more wounded.

In addition to the vast prairies, locations where miners had struck gold or silver were magnets to outlaws. They descended in hordes on the states of California, Idaho and Montana when gold was found, and were equally active around the silver mines of Nevada. Many express company stage-coaches transporting gold or silver were ambushed and robbed. The Southwest, where cattlemen grazed and drove their huge herds to market, also saw lawlessness and spates of wholesale cattle stealing. It also produced one of the most famous of all western outlaws, 'Billy the Kid'. And in the last decade of the nineteenth century, Oklahoma, with its varied landscape of uplands, lowlands, coastal plains and wooded hills, proved a profitable hunting ground for many small bands of outlaws, some white and some native American Indian, after the former Indian reserved territory, known as the 'Cherokee strip', was opened up as free land for thousands of white settlers.

A hooded bushranger holds up a traveller at gunpoint in a rugged deserted landscape.
(State Library of New South Wales)

The first Australian bushrangers, by force of circumstance, operated in Van Diemen's Land, now Tasmania, as they were escapees from the local penal settlements and had to rob to survive in the bush. Ten thousand convicts had been transported there between 1820 and 1830 and another 22,000 to New South Wales on the mainland. However, in Australia as in America, the striking of gold in Victoria immediately drew an increasing number of bushrangers to that area. The horses they used to ambush the wagons transporting the gold along deserted roads were frequently stolen from remote sheep station owners. They also robbed individuals travelling to and from the diggings and especially those on the way to Melbourne to deposit their gold. The landscape was wide and almost empty and for many bushranging became an accepted way of life.

In the early days of Victoria's gold rush, during the 1850s, robberies were particularly prevalent on the Bendigo to Melbourne road, near the Black Forest. The terrain ensured that pursuit by the forces of the law would be difficult. Even Melbourne itself was not immune, as bushrangers held up travellers on the St Kilda Road, within sight of the city centre. At the time, the city was fairly small and relatively sparsely populated and many of the roads were still nearly deserted.

Oddly, the discovery of gold, also in the 1850s, in the Bathurst district west of Sydney, New South Wales, failed to trigger an immediate epidemic of bushranging. But this was to occur in the following decade when the gold diggings were more established and many miners were making fortunes, often purely by chance. The envious bushrangers decided to share in their good fortune by robbing them. Strangely, the decade before the discovery of gold at Bathurst also produced a spate of bushranging.

The discovery of gold in Victoria and New South Wales caused a temporary halt in the exploration of Australia and about half of the continent remained unexplored in the 1850s. Bushranging was therefore restricted to the outskirts of settlements, farthest from the meagre forces of the law, and gold-mining districts. Later in the century, there were isolated instances of bushranging in Western Australia and Queensland.

COSTUME AND DISGUISE

In the eighteenth century the English highwayman wore a long-tailed embroidered coat, silk waistcoat, close-fitting breeches, white shirt, buckled low-heeled leather shoes or black leather boots with brown tops. The shirt was either richly embroidered or finished with a ruffle, this frill of lace showing at the neck and the cuffs. In fact, the dress was that of a typical English gentleman or wealthy townsman of the time.

A tricorne, or three-cornered cocked hat, was the usual headgear. Beneath the hat a wig was normally worn, although some highwaymen grew their hair long, combed back and tied in the mode of the day. Gathered together, a wig could conceal the lower part of the face. Some high-

waymen wore a black wig to hide the true colour of their hair.

Wigs, however, were not in general fashion until about 1660, so the earlier seventeenth-century highwayman could not disguise his hair in this way. Nor were tricornes worn before 1690; instead there were soft hats of various crown heights, with adjustable brims that could be pulled down to shield the highwayman's features. The footwear consisted of wide-topped boots, occasionally reaching up to the thigh.

It was imperative for self-preservation that highwaymen, no matter where, should not later be identified by their victims. Many were ruthless enough to ensure this could never happen by resorting to murder. Others simply adopted masks and disguises. The English highwayman often placed a black mask over his eyes, or sometimes a handkerchief around his mouth, as well as using his hat or wig to shield his features. One of the earliest English highwaymen, Gamaliel Ratsey, executed in 1605, wore a hideous hood

In the early days of gold mining in Victoria, Australia much violence prevailed. Prospectors had frequent fights with fellow miners in various disputes, in addition to surviving attacks from bushrangers. Picture from a John Leech cartoon.

with eye slits that covered his entire head and probably terrified his victims more than his threatening weapons. Another English highwayman of the eighteenth century, James Maclaine, donned a very elegant Venetian mask and became known as the 'gentleman highwayman' due to the very fine apparel he always wore when carrying out his robberies.

Highway robbery in England was occasionally carried out by women, who sometimes donned male clothes to disguise themselves as men. One such highwaywoman in the early seventeenth century was the notorious Mary Frith, alias 'Moll Cutpurse', who also smoked a pipe and carried a sword. A more practical reason for male disguise was that by wearing men's breeches, a woman could ride astride a horse, thus making it easier to control, especially when turning sharply or jumping an obstacle, than riding side-saddle in a skirt. Moreover, the protruding pommels of the side-saddle could inflict serious injury if the horse fell and rolled over on to its rider.

The American outlaw was more likely than his English counterpart to resort in an emergency to murder, shooting his victim with his six-gun worn high on the hip in its holster, rather than in a low-slung holster as shown in many Western movies. For disguise, he would usually tie a bandanna around his face, under a broad-brimmed hat. An exception was the famous Californian highwayman, Charles E. Boles, alias 'Black Bart', who wore a loose linen coat and a flour sack with slit-holes over his head.

In the frontier lands of the American West there was little fashion in clothes and a variety of hard-wearing garments were worn to cope with the harsh life-style. However, a few of the many professional gamblers who plagued the area dressed in more elegant clothes purchased in the east. The most famous American woman outlaw, Belle Starr, nicknamed 'The Bandit Queen', who operated in Texas and Oklahoma Indian Territory, usually dressed distinctively, if not stylishly. She clad herself either in velvet and feathers or buckskin and moccasins.

The Australian bushranger was also likely to kill his victim, especially if he was an escaped

Ned Kelly, notorious Australian bushranger, at bay from the police – despite his armour he was wounded, captured and later hanged. (State Library of New South Wales)

convict or 'bolter'. The free-born settlers, turned bushrangers, were generally less desperate. A few Australian bushrangers operating in New South Wales in the 1840s were recorded in one newspaper as being extremely gaudily dressed, drawing rather than evading attention. They wore elegant Manila hats, crafted from hemp fibres, with broad brims turned up in front and decorated with colourful ribbons. Around their necks they draped satin scarves and their coats were bedecked with many brooches. They also

Belle Starr on horseback. A notorious lady outlaw of the American West.
(Library of Congress, LC-USZ62-63912)

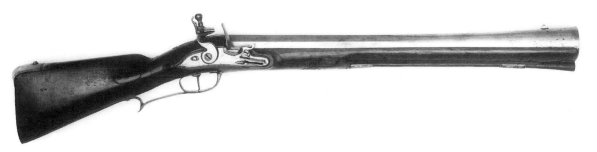

An early eighteenth-century blunderbuss with an iron barrel. Many of the early blunder-busses had long barrels which were shortened on later models. Coach and carriage passengers often carried such weapons to deter highwaymen. (Courtesy of Sotheby's)

decorated their horses' bridles lavishly with metal rings and, oddly, watches.

Even more bizarre was the attire finally adopted, prior to his capture, by the notorious Australian folk-hero, Ned Kelly: a home-made suit of metal armour, made from ploughshares, hammered into shape for him by a sympathiser. It covered both his face and body, making him look like a mock-medieval knight. His helmet resembled an inverted metal can placed over the head, with slots for the eyes. The suit, however, was not donned as a disguise but as self-protection against the forces of the law. The actual armour worn by Ned Kelly has been preserved and is exhibited in the Melbourne Museum.

Another gang of bushrangers operating in Victoria disguised their features completely by wrapping woollen scarves around their heads, apart from a small gap for the eyes. In Australia, a disguise was even more essential than in England because of the sparse population; everyone knew everybody else in their immediate neighbourhood.

Although highwaymen and women might successfully disguise themselves, it was far more difficult to disguise their horses. Even if the markings and colour of the horse were made inconspicuous, it was impossible to hide the general conformation of the animal from the experienced eye; and in those days, most people were expert in spotting a horse, as it was their sole means of transport. Furthermore, a good, speedy horse was necessary for survival and the better

the horse the more its stamp and quality would stand out.

Many of the horses used by highway robbers were stolen and their owners were bound to recognise them at a glance when seen again. Among a number of highwaymen betrayed by their horse was Dick Turpin, who once narrowly escaped the arm of the law when a bay mare he had stolen was recognised resting in a stable.

When a highwayman went on a night-time foray, the sound of his returning horse would be heard by his neighbours and therefore arouse curiosity, especially if done on a regular basis. One Lancashire highwayman in the eighteenth century overcame the problem by drawing woollen stockings over his horse's legs to muffle the clatter of the hooves when riding up a flagged alley back to its stable – a ruse imitated by many others. In this case, unfortunately, the ploy failed. He was arrested and later executed. Because his body was destined to go to a medical team for dissection, as sometimes happened at that time, he was cut down from the gallows rather prematurely. When delivered to the doctors, he showed signs of recovery and one of the medical students performed the 'coup de grâce' to become his final executioner.

AMBUSH TECHNIQUE

As is the tradition today in England, so through the centuries horse-drawn coaches and carriages have always driven on the left-hand side of the road. There were apparently two reasons for this. First, many of the English roads were narrow, with hedges and trees closely bordering each side, as many still do today in rural areas. The box-seat, where the driver sat, was on the right-hand side of the carriage and he held his driving whip across his body, from right to left, to avoid entanglement with that of a driver passing in the opposite direction. This also reduced the risk of a driver catching his whip on the bushes on his own nearside. The second reason for passing an approaching carriage or horseman right-side to right-side was that it offered a better defence for the driver in the event of sudden attack. The majority were right-handed and a sword or other weapon was therefore easier to use.

The fact that the driver of a coach or carriage was generally armed increased the hazards to the highwayman. He would normally ride out of the shadows at the base of a hill and stop the vehicle by calling out 'Stand and deliver!' or 'Your money or your life!', pointing his pistol at the driver. As the coaches drove on the left-hand side of the road, it was therefore safer for the lone highwayman to stand a little way back on the near side of the vehicle after it had been halted, so that he was out of range of a sword thrust and a more difficult target for the driver who would have to turn to fire his own pistol. The highwayman could then concentrate on the passengers inside the coach or carriage, but he was still at risk because they, too, were frequently armed. For them highway robbery was a terrifying experience and they were determined to protect their belongings – and some of them were very wealthy – at all costs. Consequently, single highwaymen were more inclined to choose prudence rather than greed, and to rob lone travellers rather than challenge a coach. Either way, survival often depended on his being very adept at the use of firearms and an excellent shot, in addition to being a bold and competent horseman.

The more cunning highwayman would sometimes adopt a different ploy. He would drive to the vicinity of his proposed ambush place, in a four-wheel open carriage drawn by one or two horses. He would then halt in a quiet, sheltered spot, unhitch one of the horses and saddle it for mounting. After changing into his professional clothes and disguise, he would depart to seek his victim. After the robbery, he would ride back to his waiting carriage, change back into his original clothes, reharness the horse in the carriage and drive home like a respectable member of the community.

As an alternative, the highwayman might pretend to be a harmless lone traveller on horseback. He would trot up to a carriage and engage the driver in friendly conversation and then travel alongside the carriage for several miles until a suitable deserted spot was reached. He would suddenly reveal his true colours by producing his pistol and carrying out his robbery. This technique, however, was risky because the carriage driver and occupants would easily be able to identify him if seen again.

When two highwaymen worked together in an ambush, one of them would stop the driver from the front, covering him with his flintlock pistol, thus screening himself from the passengers inside the coach, none of whom would risk a shot for fear of hitting the driver. Meanwhile his accomplice would approach from the rear to cover the passengers and proceed to rid them of their valuables.

In the open country of seventeenth-century continental Europe, where large bandit bands operated from hill or mountain retreats, force of numbers usually triumphed when attacking, pursuing and robbing their victims. Favourite haunts included the Sierras of Spain, the mountains of Calabria in the southern toe of Italy, the Apennines in central Italy and the highlands of Sicily, Corsica and Greece. France, too, was infested by bandits.

In general, most governments in Europe through the centuries have been much more concerned about large-scale banditry than with isolated individual highway robberies. Groups of bandits often posed a threat to their political power and survival, especially if the renegades proclaimed a nationalistic intent, thus gaining support from like-minded sections of the population.

— CHAPTER TWO —

THE VICTIMS AND THE BOOTY

Virtually any individual travelling with valuables on their person or carried by their horse, wagon or carriage was a potential victim of a highwayman or outlaw. Even money deposited in the bank was not beyond the clutches of the nineteenth-century American outlaw. Jesse James, for example, specialised in such raids. It is estimated that the James gang carried out seventeen successful bank and train robberies, with a total haul of around $200,000. They also bungled several other attempts. Jesse and brother Frank were extremely lucky to escape when robbing a bank at Northfield, Minnesota in 1876, during which their three cousins were caught, convicted and gaoled.

EUROPEAN VICTIMS

Many victims lost not only their valuables but also their lives; others suffered serious injuries. Law enforcers as well experienced many fatal casualties in their battles with the desperadoes. Only the very poor who travelled on foot had nothing to fear, as they had nothing to give, and often did their utmost to protect the bandits they admired.

Rich feudal landlords, government officials and tax-collectors were particularly hated in Europe and waylaid by the bandits, as were customs men who were robbed after they had made their seizures and confiscated goods. In eighteenth-century France these included smuggled com-

A private carriage of a wealthy family on a country road – a favoured target for the English highwayman. James Pollard engraving. c. 1835. (British Sporting Art Trust)

Stage-coaches were frequently robbed by English highwaymen. Painting by James Pollard of Robert Nelson's Red Rover, London to Brighton coach, passing a toll-gate. (British Sporting Art Trust)

modities – deer which had been poached by the poor from the king and illegally acquired salt, thus breaking the salt monopoly that prevailed in the eighteenth century. At the time, many brigands, in addition to their other activities, became unofficial smugglers and sellers of salt, infuriating the government, which tried to counter this by strengthening the gendarmerie.

BRITISH VICTIMS

In England, rich travellers, merchants, moneylenders, lawyers and members of the court were attacked, robbed and deprived of gold and silver watches, jewellery, purses, baggage, gold lace, silks and money, especially gold coins and even bills of exchange, disposed of through convenient channels. Several highwaymen travelled across the English Channel to Europe to 'fence' their ill-gotten gains: Holland was especially favoured for the disposal of diamonds and jewellery.

Before the establishment of the banking system in England, towards the end of the eighteenth century, travellers had no option but to carry large sums of money in gold or silver. Hence they always had to remain alert, especially when boarding a stage-coach at an inn. Some servants at the hostelry, who handled the pieces of baggage, would guess at those that might contain coins by their heavy weight, and pass on the information to a highwayman who would later proceed to rob the targeted passengers.

Highwaymen also robbed carriers, especially those suspected of transporting money that had been collected as taxes. In November 1692, near St Albans, one vicious gang ambushed a carrier taking such money from Manchester to London.

Despite the heavy escort, they succeeded in stealing £15,000. After the robbery, they callously stabbed sixteen of the horses and drove off the others to prevent pursuit. The same procedure was adopted by the famous seventeenth-century highwayman Captain James Hind, who shot all six horses of a carriage he was holding up. Other highwaymen took the precaution of cutting the girths and bridles of the horses, while colleagues tied up the victims.

Drovers and farmers travelling to and from markets and fairs, perhaps carrying sizeable sums of money from business transactions, were frequently attacked. So, too, were rich travellers and gamblers in the Newmarket area going to and from the races. This often happened after the restoration of the monarchy in 1660, when Charles II came to the throne. Many of his court journeyed to Newmarket on race days and were waylaid. Some, however, were lucky enough to be stopped by highwaymen of strong political persuasions who refused to rob Cavaliers (Royalists) during and after the English Civil War, 1642–51, but showed little mercy to Roundheads (Parliamentarians).

Such selectivity also occurred in Scotland during the late seventeenth and early eighteenth centuries, when Rob Roy held sway as an outlaw in the Highlands. His real name was Robert MacGregor and he gained his nickname because of his ruddy complexion and shock of dark red hair. Rob Roy is Gaelic for 'Red Robert' and he often signed himself 'Red Rob'. Before turning outlaw, he hired a band of armed men to protect his cattle herds from being stolen by members of other Scottish clans. His retainers would even guard his neighbours' herds, provided they paid him protection money.

Rob Roy embarked on his career of banditry in 1712, when his arch-rival from another clan, the Duke of Montrose, seized his lands for non-payment of a debt. The Montrose clan had previously ill-treated his wife Mary and their children, so he made a point of plundering their territory, operating in the area around Callander in the Trossachs, north of Glasgow. Rob Roy gained the reputation of a Scottish 'Robin Hood' but was

A well-dressed English aristocrat was an obvious potential victim of the highwayman due to his wealthy appearance and the fact he travelled in a private carriage.

eventually arrested. The authorities sent him to Newgate prison, pending transportation to Barbados, but at the last moment he was pardoned. Two of his five sons followed a criminal career; one died an outlaw in Paris and the other was hanged for abduction.

By and large, though, highwaymen were not selective and would often stop private carriages simply because the possession of such a vehicle suggested the owner would be wealthy and likely to have rich pickings on board. The seventeenth-century highwayman Thomas Sympson even robbed Judge Jeffreys, Lord Chief Justice of England – a very bold escapade in view of the judge's reputation for harsh sentencing of criminals. He was particularly notorious for his severe judgements in the aftermath of the Duke of Monmouth's rebellion, when he sent dozens of men to the gallows at Dorchester Assizes and other West Country courts. And in 1776 the Lord Mayor of London himself was held up at pistol point at Turnham Green.

Many a traveller prayed before setting out on a journey and some even wrote their wills in case it proved fatal. The roads leading to spa towns, such as Bath, offered a potentially rich haul whenever the elite and fashionable members of society drove there to partake of the waters. But sometimes mistakes occurred. There was one amusing incident in October 1735 when the notorious Dick Turpin tried to rob fellow highwayman Tom King. The latter apparently laughed at Turpin's demand, which threw Turpin into such a fit of rage that he threatened King's life. When matters were sorted out, they forged a partnership that lasted for two years until King was executed at Tyburn.

Money in transit to pay the army was equally at risk. For example, in the seventeenth century, John Cottington, nicknamed 'Mulled Sack' because of the large amounts of sherry he consumed, became even more infamous by holding up an army pay-wagon at the notorious Shotover Hill, at Wheatley near Oxford. The money was being transported to pay troops stationed at Oxford and Gloucester. Cottington and his companions attacked the twenty soldiers escorting the wagon when they stopped to water their horses. The highwaymen deliberately set up a din to deceive the troops into the belief they were greatly outnumbered, set them to flight and got away with £4000.

Many stage-coaches and the occasional mail-coach were also robbed. In addition, horses were frequently stolen and then used by highwaymen and outlaws to carry out their robberies. In Australia, bushrangers stole horses from the land squatters and some even stole racehorses to ensure they could speed quickly away from their victims and shake off any pursuit. Sheep stealing was also prevalent in Australia, as cattle rustling was in the American West. However, the bolder and more ambitious outlaws in the American West attempted to hold-up banks, trains and gold shipments, as did some of the Australian bushrangers. The less ambitious plundered carts and other potentially easier targets.

Mail robberies could also prove profitable, but here, too, high risks were involved. Until the beginning of the nineteenth century, the mail in England was always carried by postboys on horseback, who rode from posthouse to posthouse, usually inns along the route, where fresh horses were stabled. These stages were generally about ten miles apart and the lone riders were extremely vulnerable. The General Post Office offered sizeable rewards, even up to £200 on one occasion, for the apprehension and conviction of highwaymen who carried out such hold-ups. Between 1770 and 1777 experiments were made to design a so-called robber-proof mail cart, drawn by a horse and rider. Prototypes ranged from simple wooden carts carrying the mail in iron boxes, covered with canvas, to armoured carriages constructed entirely of thick metal and so heavy that at least two horses were needed to draw them. None was successful.

The next development was the use of a coach to carry the mail. The early types were flimsy, slow and cheaply constructed. In areas where robberies were most likely to occur, near London, for example, the mail-coach was escorted over the initial two stages of its journey by a military escort. Despite the improved security, on 29 January 1781 a successful robbery was made on the Bristol Royal Mail, when the brothers George and Joseph Weston escaped with approximately £15,000, a huge sum in those days. They halted the coach by levelling a pistol at the driver, who was forced to alight. The Westons then drove away the coach, which was later found abandoned, minus most of the mail. The Westons did not live long to enjoy their fortune but were apprehended the following year, convicted and hanged at Tyburn in 1782.

From 1784 onwards, a new type of fast mail-coach was introduced by John Palmer, who was not a post office official at the time but an influential politician and an owner of a theatre in Bath. He became disgruntled with the long time it took for both people and letters to travel between London and Bath. He suggested many procedural improvements to increase the efficiency and speed of the mail service. At first, the General Post Office were reluctant to make the changes but Palmer managed to gain the support of William Pitt, the Prime Minister of the day. The improvements then introduced later included more efficient coach designs.

The new-type mail-coach, drawn by a team of four horses, was manned not only by a driver but also an armed guard, equipped with a sword or cutlass, a blunderbuss and a pair of pistols. As always, some of the passengers regularly carried arms for their own protection. The blunderbuss, in particular, was an ideal weapon for short-range use against a highwayman. It was a muzzle-loading flintlock gun with a flared bell-shaped muzzle which fired many balls at the same time. Any deficiency in the guard's accuracy when firing under pressure was overcome by the arc of spread of the balls.

The guard always sat alone on a single seat situated on the top and at the rear of the coach, over the hind-boot carrying the mail. The boot opened at the top and the guard sat with his feet firmly on the cover. For further security, no one was allowed to sit near the guard. In any event, Post Office rules stipulated that throughout England, only three passengers were allowed to travel on top of the coach and four inside. The reason for the relatively isolated position of the guard was to prevent a potential robber, under the guise of being a passenger, becoming too friendly and talkative in order to surprise and disarm him.

An attempted attack on the new type of mail-coach in 1786, near London, resulted in failure, with the highwayman being shot dead by the guard. After this incident, few other attempts on the mail-coach were recorded by the General Post Office. Another setback for the highwaymen was that the improved roads and the turnpike system allowed the coaches to travel at much greater speeds, between seven and ten miles per hour.

Because the mail-coach displayed both the Royal Coat of Arms shield and the words 'Royal Mail' on the side, by precedent it enjoyed right of way. In addition, the upper part of the bodywork

An early nineteenth-century double-barrelled flintlock pistol that allowed two individual shots to be fired before reloading. Each barrel had its own lock and trigger. The pistol was made by Henry Mortimer & Son who manufactured many of the firearms carried by mail-coach guards. (Courtesy of Sotheby's)

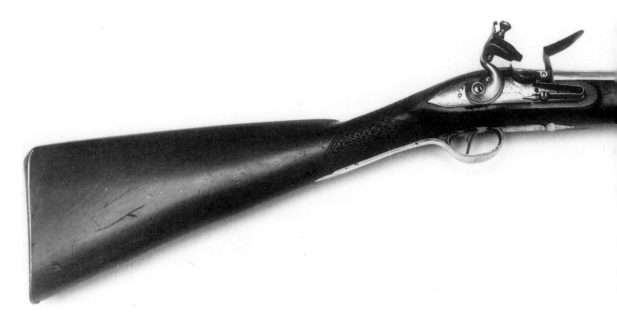

was painted black, the doors and lower panels maroon and the wheels red. The coachwork also displayed the stars of the chief knighthood orders, the Garter, the Bath, the Thistle and St Patrick. The royal cipher of the reigning monarch was always painted on the front-boot. The presence of the armed guard, reinforced by the grand display of the royal insignia, caused many a highwayman to hesitate before holding up a mail-coach.

The royal connection with the post dated back to the medieval period, when messengers were employed by the king as members of the Royal Household, to transport state letters and documents around the country. In the sixteenth century, the Royal Post started to accept a limited number of private letters, in addition to those of the state. The following century, in Charles I's reign, the system was extended so that general members of the public could send letters via the Royal Post. There was a variable fee depending on the size and distance to be carried. This continued until 1840, when the 'penny post' was introduced by Sir Rowland Hill for a single postage rate within the British Isles.

The guard gave advance warning of the approach of the mail by blowing a long straight horn, commonly known as the 'yard of tin'. In fact,

the posthorn was initially made of brass with a cylindrical bore, but later some were made of copper with conical bores. The 'yard of tin' was also used to warn toll-house keepers to open the gates and let the mail speed through. The mail-coach was exempt from toll charges, as were other specified users, such as the Royal Family, local clergy and the military. The amount to be paid to the toll-house keeper varied, depending upon the type of carriage, cart or farm animal to be driven through the turnpike gate across the road. The sums collected on a busy road could be considerable, so the keeper was always at risk from a passing highwayman. Penalties for damaging a turnpike gate were severe. An Act of Parliament of 1728 laid down a sentence of three months' imprisonment and a whipping for a first offence; a second offence warranted transportation for seven years to one of His Majesty's plantations abroad. Later the death penalty was added as a deterrent.

In the nineteenth century, the volume of mail increased to such proportions that it became impossible to carry it all in the hind-boot. Less important mail was therefore carried in large sacks on the top of the coach. By now the menace of the highwayman had been drastically reduced, so that security was less of a problem. However, the London Post Office supplied an official uniform to the guard to

A typical late eighteenth-century, early nineteenth-century blunderbuss carried by English mail-coach guards. The weapons were loaded with 9 or 10 lead balls which spread when fired to increase the chance of hitting an attacking highwayman. Such weapons were also sometimes fitted with spring bayonets. (Courtesy of Sotheby's)

AMERICAN VICTIMS

In the nineteenth-century American West, by contrast, ambushes of mail-coaches by bands of outlaws became increasingly frequent. In open country the coach would attempt to run the gauntlet, and so-called 'shotgun messengers' sat beside the driver to protect the mail. These guards were extremely competent marksmen, who stayed cool under pressure and were well capable of holding their own against most outlaws, even when the horses were galloping at speed. The bark of the six-gun and the shrill scream of the repeater rifle became frequent sounds along the trails.

Many Western pioneers had been prejudiced against the repeater rifle, complaining that it was underpowered. Although this may have been true for the buffalo hunter, it was certainly favoured later by many outlaws and guards. Earlier in the century, guards used various types of rifles and shotguns, the latter especially favoured for short-range use. The Winchester rifle of the late 1870s held fifteen cartridges and its improved accuracy

give him an air of importance and authority. This consisted of a scarlet coat, trimmed with blue lapels and blue lining, a blue waistcoat underneath, and a beaver hat with a band of gold lace.

A mail-coach was a tempting but dangerous target for a highwayman to attack because of an armed guard. Painting by James Pollard of a mail-coach in a flood near Shillingford Bridge, Berkshire, England, 1825. (British Sporting Art Trust)

Winchester rifle used by Jesse James. (Library of Congress, LC-USZ62-50009)

and rapidity of fire made it a formidable weapon.

By this time the railroads, too, were inviting targets. The outlaws halted the trains by laying logs across the track and by loosening rails at blind curves, in addition to using dynamite. One of the early train robberies in America was committed in the 1870s by the Reno gang in Indiana. This was quickly followed by Jesse and Frank James, with their confederates, who held up a train near Glendale, Missouri. The James gang next robbed a train on the Chicago, Rock Island and Pacific Railroad at Adair, Iowa. They disguised themselves as Ku-Klux-Klansmen, murdered the conductor and another railroad employee, but escaped with only $2000. Better security was later achieved by installing in the railroad cars heavy built-in safes, with time-locks or combinations that were more difficult to blow open with explosives.

Movements of gold afforded the possibility of large rewards in a single outlaw operation. Many robberies took place, especially in California during the second half of the century. The discovery of gold, on 24 January 1848, attracted the worst elements of society from as far away as Europe and Australia, who mingled with the thousands of Americans who also flooded the area. Within ten years of the first strike, nearly half a million people had arrived in the Pacific Far West.

Outlaws frequently launched attacks on the stage-coaches used to transport the gold on behalf of the express companies. For example, in 1855, 'Rattlesnake' Dick Barter and his gang robbed the Wells Fargo mule train of about $80,000-worth of gold dust. The following year, Tom Bell, known as the 'gentleman highwayman',

attempted to rob the Marysville stage of its cargo of gold worth around $100,000. The attempt failed: Bell and his gang were routed by the single shotgun messenger who valiantly fought them off. Nevertheless, between 1855 and 1869, the Wells Fargo Express Company experienced over 300 attempted stage-coach robberies.

Banks were also frequent victims of armed hold-ups. At the end of the American Civil War in 1865, any individual who met minimum standards was permitted to open a bank and offer a banking service, even though many proved financially unsound. This latitude allowed each bank to issue its own notes. Many banks were located in small, remote settlements; the outlaws simply rode into town, robbed the bank and rode out again, usually with little opposition.

AUSTRALIAN VICTIMS

In nineteenth-century Australia, with its much smaller population, only the occasional mail-coach in New South Wales was held up by bushrangers. Gold shipments and banks were far better prospects. On 20 July 1853, for instance, an armed escort departed from the McIvor gold diggings, near Heathcote, Victoria, en route to Melbourne. Within a few miles the escort was halted by a log blocking a lonely stretch of the road near an area of dense bush. While the driver and the five members of his escort attempted to move the obstacle, a fusillade of shots rang out. Three fell wounded and the others managed to escape into the bush. A dozen bushrangers then emerged from their cover, robbed the carriage and escaped with approximately 2200 ounces of gold and £700 in cash. Although this was one of the few really successful robberies of a gold escort in Victoria, it brought little luck to most of the outlaws: several of the gang were later captured, three were hanged and one committed suicide.

One of the boldest bank robberies took place on an October day in 1854 when Henry Garrett and three companions walked into the Bank of Victoria in Ballarat, about sixty miles north-west of Melbourne. The pistols they produced for the robbery were unloaded and they walked out with about £14,000. Garrett subsequently decided to sail to London to spend a life of leisure. Unfortunately, he was recognised by chance and deported back to Australia where he served a prison sentence. After release, he travelled to New Zealand and resumed his former career of bushranging.

Ned Kelly and his gang also carried out two spectacular robberies of banks. The first occurred on 10 December 1878 at the small town of Euroa,

about a hundred miles north-east of Melbourne. Before robbing the bank, the Kelly gang took over a sheep station, three miles outside the town, to water and rest their horses. One of the gang remained behind to guard the twenty-two people on the station, who were locked in a storeroom. At the same time, Ned Kelly, accompanied by two others, drove into town in broad daylight in a horse and cart. They entered the bank an hour after closing and stole £2000 in gold and notes.

About two months later they committed an even more daring robbery at Jerilderie, about a hundred miles west of Wagga Wagga, in New South Wales. They entered the town on a Saturday, took over the police station and locked up the two constables. Dressing themselves in police uniforms and stabling their horses, they spent the entire next day in town. On the Monday morning, still disguised as policemen, they

Robbery of the McIvor gold escort in Victoria, Australia. Engraving by W. Hatherall. (State Library of New South Wales)

walked into the Bank of New South Wales and escaped with over £2000 in notes and coins.

ROBBERY AVOIDANCE

In England, travellers in stage-coaches and private carriages took many precautions against the likelihood of highway robbery. The rich often travelled with armed servants as guards. A few carriages, too, were specially fitted with a sword case inside the carriage, within easy reach of the passenger, and some had convenient receptacles to carry a pistol or blunderbuss. Stage-coach proprietors, on occasion, enlisted the aid of an armed guard to protect their passengers. In 1775 the Norwich coach was stopped in Epping Forest by a gang of seven highwaymen. In the ensuing mêlée, the guard managed to shoot three of them before he was killed himself.

One ingenious resort for nervous travellers was to cut their bank notes in half and carry only one half with them, sending the other half by a separate mail-coach, with a view to reuniting safely the pieces later. Others always carried a few guineas in a separate pocket, in the event of being waylaid, in the hope that this sop would satisfy the highwaymen and avoid violence. Several carriers and travellers who passed regularly through a district occasionally paid protection money to a highwayman to ensure a safe passage through the territory he dominated. As recorded in Macaulay's *History of England*, the seventeenth-century Yorkshire highwayman, William (or John) Nevison achieved some success with this form of blackmail. Also known as 'Swift Nick', he levied a quarterly fee on the northern drovers. Apparently he was a man of his word, as those who complied were never robbed. Nevison, with his accomplices, also protected them from other thieves who might wander into the area.

Lone horsemen were more at risk than coach passengers and sometimes travelled in groups, believing there was safety in numbers. At Kensington, in the eighteenth century, a bell rang on Sunday evenings to assemble any travellers who wished to journey in company together. The surroundings were still rural, as illustrated by the fact that the Berkeley foxhound pack hunted in the vicinity. Kensington was also a dangerous area. A trial witness at the Old Bailey declared that he had seen a well-known highwayman of the 1730s, William Gordon, actually mounted on his horse inside the kitchen of an inn situated between Kensington and Knightsbridge, waiting for victims to pass. In addition, an audacious highwayman robbed King George II himself, after scaling the wall of the royal garden in Kensington. Nor did the centre of London offer immunity from the attentions of the more daring highwaymen. In 1773, Sir Francis Holbourne and his sister were robbed in their coach at St James's Square; and the Prince of Wales and the Duke of York were robbed in broad daylight in Hill Street, near Berkeley Square, a few years later.

Some travellers thought it safer to journey along the minor roads, and took precautions to defend themselves by carrying small flintlock pistols, effective at short range, in their pockets. The earliest and most common type of pocket pistol, the 'Queen Anne', was available throughout most of the eighteenth century. Its main disadvantage was the exposed lock and trigger, which could easily catch in the lining of the pocket. Some were modified with a folding trigger that lay flush with the underside of the pistol until it was cocked; and a few even had spring bayonets fitted to them, as a further line of defence in the event of a misfire. Other travellers on horseback openly displayed their weapons, such as a sword and a brace of pistols, to discourage attack.

Special pockets in coats were sometimes useful for concealing valuables, and there were other ingenious hiding-places as well. In winter it was quite common for a lady passenger in a coach to place her feet on a foot-warmer – a metal bottle filled with hot water and placed in a wooden box, often with a tapestry or an embroidered design on top of it. The foot-warmer could also be used to conceal her valuables. Sometimes she might take the added precaution of concealing a tiny pistol in the muff she used to keep her hands warm.

In early seventeenth-century France, some travellers sewed their coins into the linings of their clothes. Alternatively, they wrapped thick layers of cotton or wool thread around their coins to disguise them and then stuck several needles through the threads: the encapsulated coins were then placed in a sewing kit as additional camouflage. Another ruse was to hide valuables in the powerfully smelling ointments that were frequently carried to treat scabs and other common skin diseases.

Victims of highway robbery in England not only stood less chance of being murdered than their counterparts in other countries but were also more fortunate in another way. An ancient law relating to the 'hundreds' – subdivisions of a county with their own courts – allowed a person to claim compensation from the sheriff of the particular area in which a robbery occurred. The sum stolen had to be considerable and the claim had to be made before sunset on the day of the crime. The exact amount involved also had to be proved, which was often difficult, although if the victim was a very rich and important member of society, no doubt his word would have been accepted. In view of the many compensation payments made, it was decided by Parliament, towards the end of the sixteenth century, that only half the loss would be made good. As Sunday was considered a day of rest, a further law passed in the 1670s ruled that no compensation was payable to any travellers robbed on the Sabbath.

Younger, inexperienced highwaymen sometimes became indirect victims themselves when exploited by the more hardened criminals of the day. Young men, living in poverty, were encouraged to take to the road and even provided with a horse and weapons by their mentors. However, after their first or second successful robbery they were betrayed to the authorities by their so-called benefactors, who claimed the substantial rewards – up to £40 – on offer at the time by the government for a successful arrest and conviction.

In addition to money, the informant could also claim the highwayman's pistols and horse. If the informant was himself a former highwayman, he was spared prosecution for his past misdeeds because of his apparent repentance and show of public goodwill. The reward system was one of many factors that led to the gradual decline of

A pair of English Queen Anne flintlock pistols, c. 1740. The name Queen Anne relates to the type and not the date. Such weapons were carried by travellers for self-protection against highwaymen. The cannon barrels were unscrewed for loading and the powder and ball placed directly in the breech. (Courtesy of Sotheby's)

highwaymen in England, after their meteoric rise in numbers during the seventeenth and eighteenth centuries.

The offer of large rewards also brought results in the American West, with bounty hunters tracking down some of the wanted outlaws who had a price on their heads. In Australia, the method met with a more limited success because of the general reluctance of the public to co-operate with the authorities and police. With the demise of Ned Kelly, however, the age of the bushranger was finally over.

A later English Queen Anne flintlock pistol, c. 1780, with the lock mounted centrally in the wooden stock. This box-lock pocket type was again used for short-range defence against highwaymen. (Courtesy of Sotheby's)

An English Queen Anne flintlock pistol with the lock unusually mounted on the left-hand side of the stock, c. 1765. (Courtesy of Sotheby's)

CHAPTER THREE

THE RISE AND FALL OF HIGHWAYMEN

Bands of robbers roamed through Britain and Europe for many centuries. However, the peak era for the English highwayman was reached in the seventeenth and eighteenth centuries, whereas the outlaws of America and bushrangers of Australia came into prominence in the nineteenth century. As a rule, English highwaymen of the first half of the seventeenth century were less violent than their later counterparts. The main reason was that some were sons of wealthy gentlemen and landowners, having perhaps been indulged by their parents, and many had received a good education, as well as lessons in the finer skills of horsemanship.

When they reached manhood, their allowances often proved insufficient to finance the extravagant lifestyles to which they had grown accustomed. Although many had expectations of wealthy inheritance, they could not wait patiently for it and instead sought excitement by fanciful living and gambling at the fashionable gaming houses in London. In Georgian England, huge sums were wagered and lost at the tables, especially at the many gaming establishments in St James's Street, such as White's, Boodle's, Crockford's and Almack's. In order to pay their debts, many young gentlemen took to the road to seek rich victims to rob. Some were disowned by their families because of their depraved and wild living. A few gained reputations as 'knights of the road' but the admiration shown for them by the poorer sections of the community was misguided, due entirely to their superficial social graces and their occasional show of charm towards ladies while robbing them. In reality, all were simply common criminals who were ruled by self-interest and who preyed on anyone if they deemed it profitable. Unlike the very poor, who sometimes turned to robbery to survive, they could not even claim social injustice as their excuse for turning to crime. There was a lull in their activities when the English Civil War broke out in 1642. Most remained loyal to the king because of their family and expectations of inheritance. Many therefore joined the army to fight for the Royalists against the Parliamentarians and gained commissions.

After the war ended in 1651 in Royalist defeat, some resumed their former criminal activities as highwaymen; many of high social origin had few other options because their family estates had been ruined or seized. Moreover, they achieved a feeling of revenge by robbing supporters of Oliver Cromwell's Parliamentarian cause. Army training had also increased their skills in the arts of concealment and ambush.

Alongside them emerged a new class of highwaymen, consisting of army deserters and ex-soldiers. Born of poor parents, they had no education. In addition, many had been brutalised by the war and were uncouth, foul-mouthed and with a tendency to violence. Eventually, the majority met their inevitable fate at the hands of the hangman at Tyburn. Nevertheless, they were swiftly replaced by others and so the process continued throughout most of the following century.

THE RISE OF THE ENGLISH HIGHWAYMAN

The greatest period for English highwaymen was the fifty-year span between 1660 and 1710. So many people lived in abject poverty, drudgery and destitution that they took to the road to rob, or pursued other nefarious activities, in order to live. The ready availability to the poor of cheap gin and brandy also contributed to the problem. When drinking, they mixed with people who tempted them to commit crime, especially if they had failed in previous attempts to secure a livelihood by lawful means. The long wars with France also brought an upward surge in highway robbery due to the many disillusioned returning soldiers. As they possessed little or no money to purchase a horse, it was first necessary for them to steal one before they could take to the road: to reduce the risk of being seen on a stolen animal, a few even hired a horse for their first robbery, with the intention of purchasing one with the proceeds.

Other recruits to the criminal ranks came from those in service, such as footmen, butlers, valets and gentlemen's coachmen who envied the lifestyles of their employers and sought to emulate them. They therefore robbed the rich and the aristocracy to finance their acquired addiction for gambling and adventurous high-living. London footmen, in the early eighteenth century, gained an especially bad reputation, not only for becoming highwaymen themselves but also for acting in collusion with others of the profession to rob their employers. They passed on useful information, such as when and where their master was travelling and the probable route he would be taking.

THE FALL OF THE ENGLISH HIGHWAYMAN

Towards the end of the eighteenth century, an accumulation of factors led to a fall in the numbers of highwaymen on the English roads. In addition to the influence of the rewards system, better roads, turnpikes, toll-house keepers and armed guards on mail-coaches, a significant role was played, during the reign of George III, from the 1760s to the 1790s, by the widespread practice of land enclosure. Men cleared ancient woodlands to create land for improved grassland farming, where stock could be safely grazed by erecting fences and laying hedges to keep the animals enclosed in the fields.

The various fences used for the purpose included posts and rails, oxers and double-oxers. An oxer was a laid hedge with a ditch on one or both sides, with an oak rail to protect it. Fencing denied the highwayman the vast open landscape across which he had previously escaped. Horses

Footman lighting a 'link' (torch) to provide an early form of security lighting at the door of his master's house. However, in the eighteenth century many London footmen gained a bad reputation for working in collusion with highwaymen.

in those days were not schooled to jump fences; if an obstacle was encountered, the rider usually dismounted to find a way around it. If he attempted a jump, it would be taken from a standing position and so with little impetus to clear a tall fence. The risk to the highwayman was also increased by the larger number of horse-drawn vehicles on the roads. He could easily be trapped, with no obvious escape route, while committing his robbery, by the sudden appearance of another vehicle or rider on the scene of the crime.

Another reason for the decline of the highwaymen was the growing reluctance of magistrates to grant licences to inns which were known to be

An eighteenth-century bank cheque – the carrying of cheques instead of cash helped in the decline of the English highwayman. (Bank of England Museum)

their regular haunts. This created a problem for some landlords who advertised their inns as such, often untruthfully, in order to attract custom from curious sightseers.

The gradual establishment of the banking system in the eighteenth century also helped to clear the roads of highwaymen. At first banks were restricted to London but later they spread to the provinces. Consequently, by the end of the century, cheques and banknotes were habitually carried instead of gold and silver coins.

The final nail in the highwayman's coffin was the establishment of the Bow Street Runners, England's embryonic police force established by the Fielding brothers. In 1805 police horse patrols operated, especially at night, around the fringes of London. When a traveller was robbed, he went to the nearest turnpike gate to inform the toll-house keeper. Previously, all the keeper could do was to shout a warning through a speaking trumpet that a highwayman was suspected in the vicinity; now he would raise the alarm and bring out the Bow Street Runners in the area to give immediate pursuit. Rewards were also on offer to members of the public to assist the Bow Street Runners and co-operation was especially sought from those most likely to cross the highwayman's path, such as inn-keepers, stable owners and blacksmiths.

The establishment of an effective and well-administered police force, enjoying the support of the law-abiding section of the community made it extremely difficult for highwaymen and outlaws to operate and eventually removed their menace, not only in England but also in continental Europe, America and Australia.

THE AMERICAN WEST

In America, the westward expansion was so rapid that it was always a step ahead of a proper law-enforcing system. This often led to vigilantism, with citizens taking the law into their own hands. Although many injustices were perpetrated, such crude methods often proved highly effective in controlling outlawry. The accused was usually given a brief 'trial' by a group of 'leading citizens'. If found guilty, he was either driven out of town, flogged or hanged from a branch of the nearest convenient oak or cottonwood tree, depending upon the offence. In California, after a hanging, the victim was buried with the rope still around his neck but the end of the rope was left exposed above ground level, as a warning to other outlaws not to stay in the neighbourhood.

Law and order in America only became more established with the improvement of communications, not least the installation of the telegraph, in the remote areas of the West. Whereas in the past, information on wanted outlaws could only be sent by messengers on horseback, reliable intelligence regarding the movement of outlaws could now be swiftly transmitted to law officers. Thus far the most efficient service had been the famous Pony Express, during the period 1860–1. This operated between Sacramento in California and St Joseph, Missouri, in the Middle West, as a rival to the Overland Mail Company. Although the speed was extremely fast in terms of horse travel, it still took eight to ten days for the complete journey of 1800 miles. The horses used were ponies, endowed with speed and stamina and selected from breeds which were ideal for crossing rough terrain, such as hills and mountainous country.

The expert riders were all under eighteen years old and it was essential they were light-weight, tough and fearless. In view of their dangerous job – they often travelled through hostile Indian territory and could also be waylaid by outlaws – recruitment of orphans was generally preferred.

The wages were 25 dollars per week and for this they risked their lives daily.

The Pony Express riders rode in continuous relays between stages of nine to fifteen miles apart and there were 190 stages. The rider changed horses at each stage and just two minutes was allowed for him to vault off one horse and on to another fresh one. Pony Express riders were armed but light-weight weapons were preferred, so that the weight did not impede the speed of their mounts. The service lasted for just nineteen months. Its doom was heralded by the first transcontinental telegraph message flashed between San Francisco and Washington on 21 October 1861. The most famous of the many Pony Express riders was William Cody ('Buffalo Bill'),

to the West. Frank and Jesse James were typical examples. Both had served as Confederate irregulars, under the leadership of William C. Quantrill, against the Unionists. They had been trained in guerrilla warfare tactics – useful assets, alongside their skill with the gun, in their later outlaw activities. The end of the Civil War especially brought much lawlessness to Texas. To swell the numbers of local outlaws operating in the area, many Mexican bandits were encouraged by the absence of efficient law enforcement to cross the Rio Grande and steal cattle from the vast numbers of herds in the state.

Professional gambling, although considered quite a reputable occupation in the West, also caused many men to become outlaws when their luck ran out. During the 1860s, as the railroads expanded, linking the boom and cattle towns, gambling activity reached a climax. On the trains came a mixture of adept professional card players and the dregs of human society, looking for an easy 'buck'. The potentially explosive combination of card-playing for high stakes and the frequent heavy drinking in saloons often resulted in violence and death. However, by this time a modicum of law and order ensured that anyone involved in a fatal gun-fight had to face a coroner's court, to enter a plea of self-defence. The law officer, too, had to prove that his action was a justifiable homicide, carried out in the pursuit of duty. Many survivors of gun-fights often became outlaws and horse thieves rather than face such a court.

Cattle rustling in New Mexico proved a further boost for outlawry. Feuds between rival cattle ranchers and merchants eventually led to the Lincoln County cattle war breaking out in 1878. It was at this time that 'Billy the Kid' became

later to become the celebrated buffalo hunter and showman, after he started his Wild West show in 1883.

As had happened two centuries earlier in England, the conclusion of the American Civil War in 1865 led to many disbanded soldiers taking up a life of crime. They found it difficult to settle down again in peaceful occupations and many travelled

Cattle raid on the Texas border. A gun-fight between cattlemen and bandits. Wood engraving in 'Harper's Weekly', 31 January 1874. (Library of Congress, LC-USZ62-55596)

involved in violence, murder and rustling during the many disputes between the cattle barons. Despite being a cold-blooded killer, he gained some admiration and support from the poorer homesteaders and squatters who were dominated and badly treated by the powerful cattle ranchers.

By the end of the nineteenth century, the combination of good law enforcement and the use of the fast links provided by telephone and telegraph, greatly reduced the numbers of the horse-mounted American outlaws. One of the few survivors, Robert Leroy Parker, better known as 'Butch' Cassidy, managed to flee to England before eventually retiring to South America. Cassidy was exceptional and remarkable for a Western outlaw because he lived to a good age and never personally shot or murdered any man. The

nickname was simply due to his previous employment in a butcher's shop. He maintained his principles despite associating with many notorious outlaws, including Harry Longbaugh, alias the 'Sundance Kid'. They, with others, formed the 'Hole-in-the-Wall Gang', so named after their hide-out in the mountains whence they embarked on many train robberies along the Union Pacific Railroad. The 'Sundance Kid' also eluded the arm of the law and likewise retired to South America. It is thought that both 'Butch' Cassidy and the 'Sundance Kid' were eventually tracked down in Bolivia and killed by soldiers in 1909, although their families insisted that this was not true and that both men survived. One of the very last of the horseback outlaws was Henry Starr, related to Belle Starr, 'The Bandit Queen'. He was killed in 1921, during an attempted bank robbery. His

Saloons and disreputable places of Hazen, Nevada. June 24, 1905. Heavy drinking and gambling disputes frequently led to gun-fights and men becoming outlaws. Picture by Lubkin. (National Archives, Maryland, USA)

death finally drew the curtain on the era of the Western horseback outlaw.

THE AUSTRALIAN SCENE

In Australia the activities of the bushrangers were marked by distinct phases, interspersed with periods of relative calm. The first major outbreak occurred in Tasmania (then known as Van Diemen's Land), during the last decade of the eighteenth century and the first half of the nineteenth century. The main participants in this banditry were escaped convicts from the penal settlements, joined by a few army deserters, sailors and criminals who had served their sentences and now sought an adventurous lifestyle. The first man to escape to the bush, in 1789, was John Caesar, a First Fleet negro convict nick-

named 'Black Caesar', who had been sentenced at Maidstone, Kent, in 1785, to seven years' transportation to New South Wales. Many of the convicts transported to Australia had been found guilty of relatively minor offences but after escaping from the harsh, brutal prison settlements they drifted into a life of serious crime. Many therefore acquired further convictions. Once on the run they had to rob for sustenance and many seriously injured or killed their victims in the process. The worst offenders transported from Britain were sent to Tasmania to serve their sentence at Port Macquarie Harbour. Here, under terrible conditions, they worked like slaves felling tall trees in the rain forest and dragging the huge logs to the shore. The Macquarie Harbour prison settlement was abandoned in 1833 and a new,

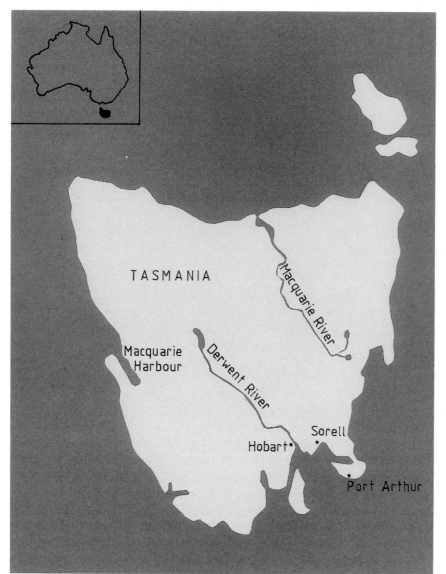

Tasmania (formerly Van Diemen's Land) – escaped convicts from the early nineteenth-century prison settlements at Macquarie Harbour and Port Arthur led to a rise in outlawry.

equally grim one opened at Port Arthur, on the south-eastern Tasmanian peninsula.

Times were very harsh and the authorities imposed extreme penalties for almost all offences. Many were sentenced to death, for example, for sheep-stealing. The Governor of Van Diemen's Land dealt severely with the escaped convict bushrangers but only gained some measure of control by proceeding to break up the organised gangs that had formed. Many members of the gangs were captured or shot evading arrest; hundreds were later executed. Although major

bushranging was suppressed in this way, several individuals still continued to operate on a small scale in Van Diemen's Land.

The early convict bushrangers – a violent breed – were regarded as a menace by the vast majority of citizens; but their successors, the Australian-born bushrangers, gained sympathy from members of the poor, tiny, outlying settlements in the bush. The later bushrangers were secretly admired because they held the police up to public ridicule, stood up as individuals against the authorities, and brought some of the richer and pompous members of society down to earth by robbing them. Many viewed their exploits as revenge for the social injustice under which they lived.

The second epoch of major bushranging took place on mainland Australia during the nineteenth century, after a period of relative calm. It came with the discovery of gold during the 1850s and 1860s in Victoria and New South Wales. Many of the bushrangers in New South Wales came from the ranks of Australian-born sons of poor settlers, although their ranks were swelled, in Victoria, by ex-convicts from Tasmania and a few work-shy adventurers. The majority of the New South Wales bushrangers preferred only to rob their victims and then disappear quietly into the bush with their booty. They only became violent when resistance was offered and therefore, in general, they were not as bloodthirsty as their ex-convict counterparts. The incidence of bushranging reached such a pitch that the authorities were forced to introduce draconian methods to control it. As well as gold shipments, individuals were robbed, horses, sheep and cattle stolen, travellers attacked and banks and post offices plundered. With each success, the bushrangers became more bold and adventurous.

Even before the discovery of gold in the 1850s corps of mounted troopers were used, together with an inadequate police force, in an attempt to control the bandits. As early as 1825, a Bushranging Act was passed by the Legislative Council of New South Wales to suppress the activity and a reward of five pounds was shortly afterwards offered as a bounty for each outlaw captured. In 1830, the Legislative Council passed a further Act, so that suspects could be arrested without a warrant by any citizen. Also, anyone found carrying firearms could be immediately arrested and suspected persons could be searched. Police, with search-warrants, could enter any house by day or night to look for firearms and if found, arrest the occupants and seize their weapons. When convicted, bushrangers were summarily sentenced to death without right of appeal and most were executed three days later. The harshness of the Act was bitterly resented by many settlers.

The severe methods, sentences and heavy-handed police action gained sympathy for the bushrangers from many members of the public, who assisted them to escape arrest by using the so-called 'bush telegraph', a term first used on 30 January 1866 in the *Sydney Morning Herald*. It entailed giving undercover information to the bushrangers on the movements of the police and warning them of an impending raid, often when the police were still many miles away. The bush telegraph was well organised and later, in other countries, it came to stand for the 'grapevine' passage of news.

As Australia became more settled and policing improved, people gradually accepted that the police were trying to defend their interests, especially if they owned property. Furthermore, the growing use of non-negotiable bank cheques often made the hold-up of travellers less profitable. Two well-known Australian bushrangers, Ben Hall and John Gilbert, were allegedly incensed when they robbed the Boorowa mail-coach in 1863 and found that most of their booty was in the form of cheques, even demanding that they be cashed by the passengers carrying them! One of the final blows against the bushrangers was the passing by the New South Wales government of the Felons Apprehension Act of 1865. This proclaimed all bushrangers as outlaws who could be shot on sight, if they did not immediately surrender their arms when challenged. Anyone giving assistance or sheltering the desperadoes were classified as felons, rather than citizens committing a minor misdemeanour.

This phase of bushranging activity ended in 1870 but the population, in general, still held grave reservations against the police, the law, officialdom and government. These antagonisms were deeply ingrained. Some Australians today are quite proud to trace their ancestry back to the convict transportation era or the days of the 'wild colonial boys'. Although major bushranging had declined, there was a minor but highly significant eruption in 1878, with the emergence of the gang led by Ned Kelly. This small group captivated the public's imagination and ensured that Ned Kelly

A convict scene in Sydney, Australia in 1830. From A. Earle's 'Views in New South Wales and Van Diemen's Land', 1830. (State Library of New South Wales)

would be the most famous and best remembered of the Australian bushrangers.

At the time, there were many unresolved tensions between small settlers and wealthy pastoralists. The Kellys lived on a small remote property and were often in conflict with the big cattlemen. Cattle stealing was rife and the Kellys were involved – angry, like many others, at the unfair and unequal distribution of land. In addition, Ned Kelly appeared to hold a pathological hatred of the police and the essential law and order required of a civilised society.

Kelly also demonstrated the seemingly inborn antipathy of the Irish Catholic towards the English Protestant. His father, John Kelly, had earlier been transported in 1841 to Van Diemen's

Land from Tipperary in Ireland, as a convict, for stealing two pigs. As a consequence, Ned concluded that no Irishman could ever expect justice in any law court in England or Australia. He was convinced that all police were hired by powerful landlords to deprive Irishmen of their land rights.

Despite Ned Kelly's violent and murderous life as a bushranger, fed by delusions of grandeur, he gained many admirers for his daring exploits and became a people's hero. His crimes have since been much romanticised, both in story and song. When he was hanged in Melbourne, on 11 November 1880, at the age of twenty-six, it brought an end to the final epoch of the Australian outlaw. His reputed last words were, 'Such is life!'

EUROPEAN BANDIT BANDS

The type of outlawry prevalent in Australia, Britain and North America differed fundamentally from that in mainland Europe. In Europe there were, of course, individual outlaws and highwaymen but there were also large bandit bands of up to one hundred horsemen. They isolated themselves from so-called organised society and occasionally even threatened established governments, especially if they were weak and unstable.

In Spain and Italy, for example, during the sixteenth century, the bandits held greater sway over some regions than the governments themselves. Many of the Spanish and Italian rural nobility also became involved in bandit activity to protect their interests by a feudal-style defiance of the state. In general, most of the bandit bands drew their strongest popular support in the localities where they operated. In Italy, where the term originated, a 'bandito' meant a man proclaimed to be an outlaw. Later the word described the large criminal gangs which operated in war-stricken areas. Alternatively, the word 'brigante' was used, meaning a partisan or irregular soldier. No matter what they were called, from the last decades of the sixteenth century onward, Italian bandits were arguably the most accomplished in Europe. In the early 1860s, for example, some two-thirds of the entire Italian army was deployed in controlling banditry in southern Italy.

In the aftermath of the many European wars that raged from the late sixteenth to the eighteenth century, outlaws were in their element. For example, banditry became a major problem after the end of the War of the Spanish Succession in 1714. Men skilled in the art of fighting and killing became unemployed soldiers and many merged their forces into criminal bands. A similar situation existed in seventeenth-century France, when there was a upsurge of persistent banditry. Large numbers of army deserters formed themselves into robber bands who roamed at will.

The problem, however, went deeper than that. Lawlessness in Europe was undoubtedly associated with the poverty and extreme hardship that so often devastated and demoralised entire communities. Agrarian distress, with resulting peasant agitation, oppressive taxation and class resentment aggravated the situation, especially in times of depression and economic crisis.

Having said that, it remains a simplistic historical view to blame outbreaks of crime solely on social conditions and the consequences of war. This explanation does a grave disservice to the masses of poor and deprived people everywhere who, over the centuries, have refused to resort to lawlessness and have chosen honest ways to survive in a harsh and often ruthless social environment.

Although many bandits sheltered under the cloak of social rebellion, the majority were common criminals and murderers who joined the robber bands to save themselves from punishment and the gallows. Many were villains with selfish motives who betrayed their companions and leaders to the authorities out of self-interest. They were eventually brought to book by the development of capable European administrative governments, the tightening of boundaries between states, severe penalties for criminal offenders and improved rural policing, supported by the law-abiding sections of the community.

CHAPTER FOUR

THE LAW ENFORCERS

In London, until the latter part of the eighteenth century, there was no centrally organised police force. A bill introduced to Parliament in 1785 with this aim was defeated because most members felt it would infringe upon their liberty and resisted it. In Paris, by contrast, the lieutenant of police already possessed jurisdiction over the whole city and crime was therefore easier to combat. Nevertheless, in the rest of France and throughout eighteenth- century Europe, there existed few systems of effective or centralised policing. As a consequence, governments frequently reinforced their inadequate local police forces with troops.

The parish constables, beadles and nightwatchmen who undertook the policing role in London were quite incapable of imposing order. They functioned on a purely parochial basis under local magistrates. Each parish, covering a defined area, with its church, was responsible for its own administration. The parish constables, who were householders, patrolled the local neighbourhood but they were amateurs and normally only served for one year. During their period of office, they still continued their own profession or trade and most, unless particularly public-spirited, therefore tried to avoid their mandatory spell of constable service. Some accepted the job and then paid a deputy to do it for them; others gained exemption, or a reduction in their year's service, by earning a so-called 'Tyburn ticket'. This was awarded after they had successfully brought to justice an offender who was expected to be sent to Tyburn for execution.

When on duty, the constables were not issued with uniforms but were armed with wooden truncheons, often elaborately decorated to give the bearers an air of officialdom. To assist them, the beadle who was a minor officer of the parish, took on some of their administrative functions, such as the Poor Laws and acting as town crier. In addition, the beadle supervised the watchmen who were recruited and paid by the local parish to patrol the streets during the hours of darkness. To finance this, a 'watch rate' was levied on the citizens of the parish.

'CHARLEYS'

The London watchmen became known as 'Charleys'. The reason for this is unclear, but the name probably arose after 1640 when Charles I improved and extended the night-watch system in London. The 'Charleys' were low-paid and many were old; they undertook the duty because they were unable to get another job. Each watchman patrolled an allocated street, supposedly every hour, from his sentry-box.

In 1735, the wealthier districts of London started to recruit larger numbers of watchmen, to check that house and shop doors were safely locked during their patrols. The watchmen were often tormented and sometimes attacked because they represented the law. Young men would creep up behind the sentry-boxes and push them over with the 'Charleys' trapped inside. Another favourite prank was to discover a 'Charley' having a nap in his box and awaken him with a loud bang. As a consequence, when on duty the watchmen carried wooden clubs or staffs for their own protection, as well as lanterns and sometimes wooden rattles to raise the alarm.

THIEF-TAKERS

Although this medieval-style policing system had some merit in involving the local population in

Eighteenth-century London watchmen, commonly known as 'Charleys'.
They patrolled the streets after dark to provide security.

parish law enforcement, it was completely ineffective in tracking down criminals, such as highwaymen, across parish boundaries. To alleviate
the situation, groups of unofficial 'thief-takers' or
'bounty hunters', motivated by the rewards
offered by the government for the apprehension
and conviction of offenders (£40 for a highwayman), began to operate. The 'thief-takers' also
investigated robberies, when requested, on behalf
of victims, and claimed rewards of about half the
value for returning stolen property to them.
Unfortunately, the system was abused by entre-
preneurial criminals who organised the robbers,
acted as 'receivers' of the stolen goods and then
betrayed the offenders to the authorities for
reward.

One of these unsavoury characters was
Jonathan Wild, ostensibly a zealous London
magistrate and a figure of respectability but
actually a receiver of stolen goods on an immense
scale. He also planned and organised robberies
for countless thieves and highwaymen. He set up
gangs in different areas of the country, mainly
employing men who had returned from the
colonies after transportation. Some of these
gangs were mobile and followed the royal court,
the law circuits and country fairs over much of
England. Wild controlled them by blackmail,
under the threat of exposure to the authorities,
and thus, in effect, ran a 'protection racket'. They
were completely at his mercy, unable to give evidence against him due to their criminal past;

moreover, he could have them arrested whenever he liked. If they disobeyed or rebelled, he informed on them; his double-dealing sent over sixty highwaymen and thieves to the gallows throughout the country.

Wild thus gained the grandiose title of 'Thief-taker General of Great Britain and Ireland' and tried, though unsuccessfully, to become a freeman of the City of London for his public services. He walked the streets with a short silver staff, as a badge of authority, using this to remove any suspicion were he found in the vicinity of a highway robbery which he had organised. Because of his reputation, highwaymen who did not enjoy his 'protection' gave London a wide berth in the period 1723–5, as evidenced by the fact that no highwaymen were hanged at Tyburn during this time.

Jonathan Wild's journey to Tyburn for his execution in 1725.

Jonathan Wild, known as the 'Thief-taker General of Great Britain and Ireland'. He pretended to be on the side of the law but in fact was a ruthless criminal.

Eventually, Wild's luck ran out and he was charged with several offences. He was found guilty of handling some fine Flanders lace, known to be stolen by one of his confederates, and obtaining a reward by returning it to the owner. Aged forty-three, he was executed at Tyburn in 1725. It was rumoured that at the execution he even picked the pocket of the ministering clergyman and removed a corkscrew from it! On his way to the gallows the route was lined with thousands of angry spectators who yelled for him to be 'promptly despatched' and hurled abuse, pelting him with missiles because of his treacherous and odious dealings on both sides of the law. He was buried in St Pancras churchyard. A few nights later his corpse was stolen by body-snatchers, presumably on behalf of surgeons, and his skeleton was later presented by a doctor to the Royal College of Surgeons of England and exhibited in their museum in Lincoln's Inn Fields, London.

BOW STREET RUNNERS

The first serious suggestions for overcoming the grave deficiencies of the system for apprehending criminals were made by Henry Fielding, the novelist and dramatist, after his appointment as magistrate for Westminster and Middlesex in 1749. Two years later, when senior magistrate at Bow Street, he wrote his *Enquiry into the Causes of the Late Increase in Robbery*. He concluded that the principal causes of the increase in the crime rate, including highway robbery, were gambling, cheap gin and 'the increase in luxury among the lower orders of the people'. He recommended two main remedies to improve the justice system; the recruitment of a special police force at Bow Street's magistrates' office and the offer of £100 rewards for the capture of highwaymen and other criminals.

Henry Fielding was assisted in his magistrate's role by his younger half-brother John, who continued the work after Henry died in 1754, even though he had earlier been blinded in an accident, when only nineteen years old. He was nicknamed the 'Blind Beak' and generally wore a black band around his eyes. His keen sense of hearing reputedly enabled him to recognise 3000 thieves by their voices.

In the initial stages, the special police force at Bow Street consisted of just six or seven 'thief-takers'. They were recruited from the parish constables, after their year of office had expired, were paid one guinea a week and were also rewarded when they captured or broke up a gang of highway robbers, the money they claimed becoming known as 'blood money'. At first, they wore no uniform but only carried the staff of a parish constable.

The 'thief-takers' who patrolled the streets were subsequently named the Bow Street Runners, and they were supported by increased government money. This enabled John Fielding, in 1763, to establish an experimental nightly horse patrol of eight men to protect travellers on the roads around London against highwaymen. The following year, the government withdrew this financial support and the horse patrols ceased. The foot patrols continued and although John Fielding died in 1780, six more offices similar to Bow Street were opened by 1792. In addition, another magistrate, Patrick Colquhoun, set up the Thames or Marine Police, a further step in the direction of an organised police force.

The Bow Street Runners' horse patrol was not re-established until 1805, when Sir Richard Fox set up a force of fifty to sixty men at the Bow Street police headquarters. The Bow Street Runners then became official and a uniformed horse patrol was formed to protect the principal roads within a twenty-mile radius of London. The main objective was to clear notorious spots, such as Hounslow Heath, of highwaymen so that travellers could undertake journeys with less trepidation. The police action met with huge success. On occasions, when short of men, the Bow Street Runners persuaded the military to help them tackle large groups of highwaymen.

The Bow Street Runners wore red waistcoats on duty and thus became known as the 'Robin Redbreasts'. When patrolling the streets, they carried, as badge of office, a wooden tipstaff, in the form of a short mace, on top of which was a metal receptacle containing the rolled-up warrant of arrest. They also carried thirteen-inch-long truncheons, bearing the name Bow Street and gilded with the monarch's cipher, a lion and a crown.

The success of the Bow Street Runners in suppressing the menace of the highwaymen encouraged Sir Robert Peel, when Home Secretary, to recruit greater numbers of uniformed policemen. In London, in 1822, they became known as 'bobbies', after his first name, while those he formed in Ireland in 1814 were called 'peelers'. In 1829, the Metropolitan Police Act was passed which brought all the separate London forces under a central control and the result was the establishment of the Metropolitan Police Force.

Wooden gaolhouse in Wyoming Territory. By C. Hart Merriam, 1893. (National Archives, Maryland, USA)

AMERICAN FRONTIER

In America, the situation was entirely different because the areas to be policed were immense and westward expansion proceeded well ahead of official peace officers and regular courts of law. In the early days of the mining and cattle boom towns, there were no prisons in which to lock up outlaws. Later, simple wooden buildings were used to incarcerate them. Lawmen, when they eventually reached the frontier regions, also encountered great difficulties after capturing and escorting their prisoners across country on horseback. Most had little option but to chain their captives to trees or wagons.

These factors encouraged the vigilantes to form illegal posses to hunt down desperadoes and rustlers. Unfortunately, this often entailed vio-

lent revenge rather than justice, even when a judicial system became established. Later, sheriffs and peace officers formed legal posses by calling together a group of men to assist them. They played a major role in bringing law and order to the Frontier West. Great weight of numbers was brought to bear in certain cases. In 1876, for example, a 400-strong posse rode out to kill one member and capture two others of the Jesse James gang.

American bounty hunters undertook to bring in outlaws in order to claim rewards offered by the sheriff's office. They were paid when their claim was authenticated. Once established in the West, the sheriff and his deputies were responsible for enforcing the local laws in their county. They worked in conjunction with federal marshals who were essentially under the jurisdiction of the federal district courts. Their duties were mainly administrative whereas it was the deputies who risked their lives actually enforcing the law in the field. Unlike the county sheriffs, the federal marshals and their deputies were concerned primarily with federal law violations, such as mail robberies, that affected the whole country. In addition, there were town marshals, appointed by the local mayor or council of a town, of whom the best-known were probably 'Wild Bill' Hickok and Wyatt Earp.

'WILD BILL' HICKOK

'Wild Bill', whose real name was James Butler Hickok, earned his reputation first as deputy marshal at Fort Riley, Kansas and later during 1869–71 as marshal at Hays City and Abilene, also in Kansas. The cow town of Abilene, at the end of the Chisholm Trail, over which Texan cattle were moved to meet the railroad, was a particularly violent place. Hickok served there for just eight months with great success, then left to tour eastern America with 'Buffalo Bill' Cody's Wild West Show in 1872.

Hickok had earlier gained a formidable reputation for his dexterity with the gun and this stood him in good stead in his role as marshal. The first memorable incident was his gun fight along the Oregon trail, at Rock Creek Stage Station, Nebraska with the David McCanles gang, in which he killed McCanles and two of his accomplices.

His great skill and speed with the gun were again demonstrated later in an unusual gun duel on the public square of Springfield, Missouri – unusual in the sense that both gunmen appeared to stand a fair chance of winning, rather than one of them being furtively killed, as commonly happened, by a shot in the back. Hickok's adversary was David Tutt, another expert pistol shot, as a consequence of an earlier argument over a game of poker. The men eventually squared-up when about fifty yards apart, and both were reported to draw from their holsters and fire at the same time. David Tutt's shot missed its target, while

Hickok's hit his adversary in the heart, killing him instantly.

Tutt's armed friends, who watched the duel, dispersed immediately, obviously impressed by Hickok's skill with the gun. Hickok was arrested and charged with the killing but was found not guilty on the grounds of self-defence. Although fortunate on this occasion, his good luck deserted him tragically when playing another poker game in a saloon on 2 August 1876 at Deadwood, South Dakota. Then aged thirty-nine, he was shot in the back by Jack McCall, a vagrant, who was arrested, convicted and later hanged.

WYATT EARP – MARSHAL

Like 'Wild Bill' Hickok, Wyatt Earp earned his reputation as town marshal of Dodge City, Kansas, a hotbed of violence after 1872, when it was reached by the Santa Fé railroad. It then developed as a centre for buffalo hunters who used the railway to transport thousands of hides. In the 1880s, Dodge City also became a shipping centre for cattle and brought a big influx of wild cowboys.

In the lawless early days, Dodge City saw over a score of murders take place during a period of just a few months. The local cemetery was named Boot Hill, a graveyard for men who died with their boots on. In order to enforce some kind of order, the citizens looked to expert gunmen, such as Wyatt Earp, 'Doc' Holliday, 'Bat' Masterson and William Tilghman, who all visited the town at various times.

Wyatt Earp arrived in Dodge City in 1878 to become assistant marshal and proved himself to be a very capable lawman. Here he became a close friend of 'Bat' Masterson, Luke Short and, most especially, 'Doc' Holliday, who once saved his life in the town when he was surrounded by a crowd of threatening cowboys. One of the mob drew a gun behind Earp's back, but was quickly disarmed by Holliday. The paths of the two men were later to cross again at Tombstone, Arizona, when Earp became deputy sheriff there.

Luke Short and 'Bat' Masterson also found their way later to Tombstone. The former, a noted 'fast draw' with his gun, was an expert gambler and former whiskey peddler to the Indians. Masterson was later to become one of the great frontier law enforcers, on a par with Earp, Hickok and Tilghman.

Tombstone had become a boom town in 1879 with the discovery of silver. The prospect of easy money attracted a host of gamblers, faro players, dance-hall girls, pimps, thieves and gunmen to the saloons. Faro was a particularly popular card-game in the saloons. The town and its surroundings had been noted for violence even before the silver strike, with cowboys rustling cattle in from Mexico, and afterwards became the most lawless spot in the American West.

Wyatt Earp and his four brothers, Virgil, James, Warren and Morgan, arrived in Tombstone with the intention of settling there. They invested in property and other business ventures. One of Wyatt's first jobs before becoming deputy sheriff was that of shotgun messenger for Wells Fargo. He then acquired an interest in a gambling saloon, called the Oriental, and employed 'Bat' Masterson and Luke Short to work as dealers. He also ran a faro game at another establishment, the Eagle Brewery. Meanwhile, Virgil had accepted the job of deputy marshal for South Arizona and later he also became town marshal of Tombstone when the previous holder of the post, Fred White, was shot.

All was to change when a feud gradually built up between the Earps and the lawless cowboy factions who had previously roamed at will and indulged in wild behaviour throughout the area. The feud was sparked off by the death of Fred White, shot by one of the cowboys on a rampage through the town. Wyatt, as deputy sheriff, disarmed the assailant and later, with the aid of his brothers Virgil and Morgan, arrested some of the other members of the gang. The memory of this incident caused future friction between the Earps and the cowboy gangs, comprising the Clanton and the McLaury families. The final incident, leading to the famous gunfight at the OK Corral, was the robbery of a stage-coach, with the killing of the driver and a passenger. The Earps tried to implicate associates of the Clantons, although another strong suspect was 'Doc' Holliday, who

had earlier travelled to Tombstone, hoping that its dry atmosphere would improve his health, as he suffered from tuberculosis. Although there was insufficient evidence to convict Holliday, the suspicion that he was involved persisted, and his friendship with Wyatt damaged the Earp family's reputation.

The Clantons made threats against the Earps and one of the sons, Ike, was arrested by Virgil when he tried to cause trouble by spoiling for a fight in town. At the same time, Wyatt had a confrontation with Ike's friend, Tom McLaury, and hit him over the head with a gun. A final showdown between the Earps and Clantons became inevitable. There were strong rumours that the Clantons were out to kill the Earps. Virgil, as town marshal, set out to arrest them, accompanied by his deputies Wyatt, Morgan and 'Doc' Holliday, who carried a sawn-off shotgun under his frock-coat.

The arrest was attempted at about two o'clock on 26 October 1881, in Tombstone's Fremont Street. The Clanton and McLaury brothers, with their friend Billy Claibourne, were heading for the nearby OK Corral, to collect their horses. All of a sudden violence exploded. There was frenzied shooting at close range and within a minute Billy Clanton and Frank and Tom McLaury were dead. Virgil and Morgan Earp suffered gunshot wounds in a shoulder and leg respectively, and 'Doc' Holliday nursed a bullet wound in his hip. Wyatt Earp escaped unharmed, as were Ike Clanton and Billy Claibourne who both fled for their lives from the scene.

After the bloody confrontation, the popularity of the Earps declined even further. Certain citizens complained that they had given little chance to the Clantons and McLaurys; a few even accused them of murder but the fact that two of the Earps and 'Doc' Holliday had been wounded during the fight did not give strong credence to this theory. A judicial enquiry was held and the Earps and Holliday were exonerated, the verdict being they were carrying out their duty as law officers.

A vendetta of shootings and revenge killings swiftly followed. In November 1881 Virgil was shot in the arm as he left the Oriental saloon. He never recovered movement in the arm but despite this crippling handicap he still rose to become marshal when he subsequently moved to California. Four months later, Morgan was shot in the back as he played pool in a saloon. Wyatt and Holliday then embarked on a revenge mission; after killing two of the men they suspected of murdering Morgan, they departed from Tombstone and left Arizona.

'DOC' HOLLIDAY

'Doc' Holliday remains an enigma. Curiously, despite his somewhat shady reputation as a quick-tempered gunman, likely stage-coach robber, heavy drinker and gambler, he was always on the scene to risk his life for the law when Wyatt Earp or his brothers needed assistance.

John Henry Holliday was born in Georgia in 1851 of a reasonably wealthy family and brought up with the polite manners of a Southern gentleman. When his father returned after service as an officer in the Civil War, the family moved to a new home in Georgia, but shortly afterwards his mother died and his father remarried. John Henry then left home and studied dental surgery at Pennsylvania College, graduating in 1872. He practised dentistry for a while but, at the age of twenty-two, developed a persistent cough that was diagnosed as pulmonary tuberculosis. He travelled west to Dallas in Texas and briefly continued his career, but perhaps because of his ill-health and the fear of a short life expectancy he sought excitement, drank heavily and became an extremely skilful player of faro and poker. Inevitably, as a professional and successful gambler in the West, he became involved in several shooting incidents and quickly moved from town to town, until he drifted into Dodge City.

By now he was accompanied by his common law wife Kate, nicknamed 'Big Nose' Kate. After the episodes that cemented his close friendship with Wyatt Earp in Dodge City, he moved on again, turning up in Las Vegas, where he bought an interest in a saloon. The venture soon collapsed when the 'Doc' killed a man who attempted to wreck his bar. Holliday next moved to Tombstone and renewed his friendship with Wyatt Earp and his brothers, culminating in the fight at the OK Corral.

After leaving Arizona with Wyatt Earp in 1882, both men journeyed to Denver and resumed their friendship with 'Bat' Masterson. Shortly afterwards, Holliday was arrested and nearly sent back to Tombstone to face murder charges for his part in the earlier revenge killings. Thanks to the influence of Masterson and powerful political friends of Wyatt Earp, the authorities dropped the charges. The 'Doc' then continued to drift, drink, cough and gamble, shooting another man dead in a quarrel over the card table. By this time his health had deteriorated gravely and shortly afterwards he was admitted to a sanatorium in Glenwood Springs, Colorado, for treatment of his advanced tuberculosis. He never recovered and died there in 1887 at the age of thirty-six. His wife Kate eventually remarried and settled down to run a boarding house in Arizona; a quiet life in comparison to the turbulent one she had led with the 'Doc'.

WYATT EARP – FAMILY LIFE

Wyatt Earp was born in 1848, a member of a large, close-knit family. He had four brothers, a sister who was the youngest of the family, and an older half-brother. They grew up in Illinois and Iowa but the wanderlust of their father, Nicholas, led the family, in 1864, to migrate west to California, where Wyatt and his brother Virgil became teamsters. Four years later the family moved back to Illinois before going on to Missouri. Wyatt and Virgil worked briefly on the Union Pacific Railroad, where Wyatt learned to become an expert card-gambler, and eventually rejoined the family in Missouri. Wyatt married for the first time in January 1870 and worked for a while as a lawman, but tragically his wife died the following year of typhoid. In search of adventure, he moved into Indian Territory, was accused of horse stealing but managed to escape into Kansas in 1872 to work as a buffalo hunter.

Earp then drifted from town to town and on two separate occasions worked successfully as a law-

Dodge City, Kansas, Peace Commissioners. L to R: Chas. Bassett, W. H. Harris, Wyatt Earp, Luke Short, L. McLean, Bat Masterson, Neal Brown. By Camillus S. Fly, c. 1890. (National Archives, Maryland, USA)

man. However, the wanderlust inherited from his father drove him to set out in search of gold when the rush to the Black Hills, Dakota, took place in 1877. After a subsequent short spell of gambling in Texas, he arrived in Dodge City in 1878 where he became assistant marshal and married for the second time. By 1879, things had quietened down and Wyatt departed with his wife to Las Vegas and then to Tombstone where he was reunited with his brothers and 'Doc' Holliday. Thereafter he continued his restless travels, from boom town to boom town, opening a gambling hall in San Diego in 1889. He later worked as a bodyguard and in 1896 refereed the world boxing championship fight involving the great Bob Fitzsimmons.

The following year he left for the Alaskan gold-fields and opened a saloon with his wife. After several other changes of scene, he finally settled down in Los Angeles, where he spent the rest of his life. He invested in many speculative mining ventures, without much financial success. He also became friends with Tom Mix, the early Hollywood movie cowboy star, and assisted him in his career with his knowledge and experience of the Frontier West. Wyatt Earp died on January 13 1929 at the age of eighty-one, a remarkable age for a man who had led such an adventurous and dangerous life. He once observed that the survivor in a shoot-out would always be the man who was deliberate, took his time and only had to pull the trigger once, echoing the words of 'Wild Bill' Hickok who advised, 'Whenever you get into a row be sure and not shoot too quick. Take time, I've known many a fellow slip up for shooting in a hurry.' Wyatt Earp might have added that it also took a cool nerve and a great deal of courage.

The early frontier law enforcers in the American West were mainly charismatic individuals who drifted in and out of this dangerous role. All ran risks and took jobs that could earn them a quick dollar. Almost all indulged in buffalo hunting at some stage or joined the gold rushes. The majority were enthusiastic and proficient gamblers at cards. Although at times most of them had dabbled with unlawful pursuits such as horse-thieving, the fact that they accepted posts as marshals indicated, by and large, that they chose to be on the right side of the law. Further examples of such individuals were 'Bat' Masterson and William Tilghman.

'BAT' MASTERSON

William Barclay Masterson was born in 1853 in Canada but grew up in Illinois. When he was eighteen years old, his family moved to Kansas and 'Bat', as he was nicknamed, became a buffalo hunter, together with his brother. In 1873 he got involved in a desperate fight with Indians when his hunting group was ambushed. 'Bat' reputedly showed remarkable coolness and courage in the encounter, qualities that were to serve him well

in later life as a lawman. His first spell of duty as such was in 1876 when he briefly became deputy marshal of Dodge City. He then left to join the gold rush to Deadwood, South Dakota, and on return the following year became the sheriff of Ford County.

In 1878, his brother was killed when serving as acting marshal in Dodge City and 'Bat' took immediate revenge by shooting both his assailants at the scene of the incident. He assisted Wyatt Earp in his gambling ventures and law duties when in 1880 they met in Tombstone, and he, too, became interested in boxing and other sports. 'Bat' married Emma Walters in 1891 and continued his gambler's life but later moved to New York to work as a sports writer.

President Theodore Roosevelt persuaded Masterson to become a federal deputy marshal in 1905 but two years later 'Bat' resigned and returned to journalism. He became sports editor of New York's *Morning Telegraph*. and died at his desk there in 1921 at the age of sixty-eight. His opinions on the art of survival in the Frontier West were similar to those voiced by Wyatt Earp and 'Wild Bill' Hickok: 'Always have your gun loaded and ready and never reach for it unless you are dead earnest and intend to kill the other fellow. The main thing is to shoot first and never miss. Never try to run a bluff with a six-gun. Many a man has been buried with his boots on because he foolishly tried to scare someone by reaching for his hardware.'

'BILL' TILGHMAN

The other great law enforcement officer, William Mather Tilghman, was born in 1854 in Iowa and grew up in Kansas. After a few spells of lawlessness in his early days, he became the longest-serving lawman in Kansas and Oklahoma and one of the best. At the age of sixteen, he went West and worked as a buffalo hunter. At twenty he joined a gang who stole horses from the Indians. After several narrow escapes, he left for Dodge City and for a short time took the job of a deputy-sheriff, before opening a saloon there. In 1878, he was arrested twice, first for train robbery and then for horse-stealing, but was found not guilty on both charges. He settled in Dodge City and gradually built up the reputation of an honest and respected citizen, culminating in his appointment as town marshal from 1884 to 1886.

When the former Indian reserved territory in Oklahoma was opened up as free land for white settlers in April 1889, Tilghman joined the rush. He established a claim there, after first serving for another short spell as a lawman. He later became a federal deputy marshal and enjoyed success in helping to catch many of the most notorious Oklahoma outlaws, including Bill Doolin and his gang. In this task Tilghman was assisted by marshals Chris Madsen and Heck Thomas, and the trio became known as the 'Three Guardsmen'.

Bill Tilghman respected the rights of outlaws when they were under arrest and fought hard against those who favoured 'lynch law'. From 1900 to 1904, he served as sheriff of Lincoln County in Oklahoma. He then undertook other law enforcement tasks before eventually becoming the police chief of Oklahoma City in 1911. Against the wishes of his wife, he came out of retirement in 1924, at the age of seventy-one, to become marshal of Cromwell City in Oklahoma. This proved a tragic decision, as Tilghman was murdered shortly afterwards by the drunken Wiley Lynn, who shot him twice while resisting arrest.

TEXAS RANGERS

As well as the marshals and sheriffs, the Texas Rangers played a highly significant role in controlling outlawry in that state. The Rangers, a semi-military organisation, were originally formed in 1823 to scout the movements of hostile Indians, such as the Comanches. They continued this duty for many decades, protecting Texas settlers. However, after the end of the American Civil War in 1865, the total strength of the Rangers was drastically reduced when a new state police force was established in Texas. This proved ineffective and in 1874 a special force of Texas Rangers was formed to combat the large numbers of outlaws and Mexican cattle rustlers in the state. At the same time, a Frontier Battalion of Texas Rangers was formed for service against the Indians. In 1881, they defeated the last of the Indian resistance in the Diablo Mountains of western Texas.

In their increasingly successful battle against the outlaws, the Rangers operated with ruthless efficiency and courage, assisted by formidable fire-power. This came with the development of Samuel Colt's revolver, known as the Colt Peacemaker; it had a calibre of 0.45 with a seven and a half-inch-long barrel. Each Ranger was armed with two revolvers. Among their many successes was the capture of the notorious Texas outlaw, John Wesley Hardin, in 1877 and, in the following year, the killing of the equally celebrated Sam Bass, after a shoot-out at Round Rock, a few miles north of Austin, Texas.

The Texas Rangers were greatly feared by outlaws and even the Jesse James gang kept well clear of them. The great success of the special force finally led to their redundancy in 1881 but the Frontier Battalion continued until 1901. The service was then reorganised and renamed the Texas Ranger Force to cope with the different challenges of the new century. The Rangers were modernised again in 1935 and today they remain the oldest law enforcement agency in America.

PINKERTON
NATIONAL DETECTIVE AGENCY

When the Texas Rangers shot the outlaw Sam Bass, they beat another law-enforcing body to the task. This was the Pinkerton National Detective Agency, which had been employed by the Texas and Pacific Railroad Company to track down Bass, who had robbed several of their trains and offices. The agency, founded in the early 1850s by Alan Pinkerton, an immigrant from Glasgow, Scotland, was the first American private detective agency. Then aged thirty-one, he had earlier worked as a detective for the Chicago police and as a US special mail agent. Although headquartered in Chicago, Pinkerton agents, after gaining an excellent reputation for solving a series of robberies, worked throughout America. They also organised an intelligence service for the Federal States during the Civil War. Later, they played a prominent role as strike-breakers, particularly in their battle with the unions in the eastern coal industry.

Alan Pinkerton was the first person to devise the 'rogues gallery' system, by building up a collection of detailed descriptions of known criminals. He met with considerable success in the West in his pursuit of outlaws, although the agency had a few failures and several of their detectives were killed in the process. One was murdered in 1874 while trying to work undercover against the Jesse James gang, who subsequently killed a second agent. A year later Pinkerton agents believed they had tracked the gang down to their hide-out cabin. They fired into the building but tragically killed an eight-year-old boy and wounded his mother. The victims were relatives of the James clan who had left the cabin prior to the attack. Jesse James vowed to avenge the death and tried unsuccessfully to assassinate Alan Pinkerton, even following him in Chicago for several months, awaiting an opportunity that never arose. In fact, Jesse James himself was assassinated by a member of his own gang in 1882, two years before Alan Pinkerton died of natural causes. After the death of Alan, his two sons, William and Robert, ran the agency.

Pinkerton detectives were successful in tracking down the notorious Texan outlaw gang led by the brothers Rube and Jim Burrows. In 1888, they shot down both of them and arrested the other three members of the gang. The Pinkerton Agency was also responsible for the flight of 'Butch' Cassidy and the 'Sundance Kid' to South America. They had harassed and pursued the 'Hole-in-the-Wall' gang, otherwise known as the 'Wild Bunch', for a considerable time before chasing them out of Wyoming and Montana.

Law enforcers in the West were strongly supported by the judiciary. Judges passed severe sentences and many, like Isaac C. Parker, sitting on the Fort Smith, Arkansas, federal bench, gained the reputation of being 'hanging judges'. Their philosophy, presumably, was that if you hang them, they cannot re-offend and claim more innocent victims.

AUSTRALIAN LAW ENFORCEMENT

In Australia, in the colonial days of the eighteenth and early nineteenth centuries, the task of law enforcement was mainly carried out by the military. The Governor mustered military parties and strengthened them with armed settlers in large-scale man-hunts for the gangs of bushrangers. Rewards were on offer for the capture of each one. The prevailing judicial system was that established by the British in 1787 after the First Fleet, consisting almost wholly of convicts and their guards, arrived in Botany Bay from England.

The Criminal Courts consisted of a judge-advocate, who presided with six officers of His Majesty's Forces, usually from the military garrison, although, when a warship was in port, the British Navy supplied officers as well. Any appeals against the court's decisions were made directly to the Governor. Unfortunately, most of the early judge-advocates possessed little legal training and this led to many injustices. In 1790, one such judge was Richard Atkins, a habitual drunkard who 'pronounced sentences of death in moments of intoxication'. These were the words of William Bligh, captain of HMS *Bounty*, on whose ship the famous mutiny occurred in 1787. Bligh and eighteen officers were set adrift in a small boat without maps. Bligh survived, reached safety and later became Governor of New South Wales.

The early Criminal Courts resembled court martials rather than English Courts of Justice. As a consequence, the system was reorganised between 1810 and the early 1820s when magistrates were established in the colony. The Governor then selected two of them in rotation to sit under a Chief Justice who had had legal training in England. Shortly afterwards, trial by jury was introduced and the country progressed slowly from early colonialism towards its own nationhood.

Although a police force was established in the early nineteenth century, the military still

Left: An Australian trooper in full-dress uniform on horseback in Melbourne, Victoria, c. 1861. Military troopers assisted police constables in the pursuit of bushrangers. Pencil sketch by William Strutt. (State Library of New South Wales)

bushrangers. They also employed aborigine trackers to lead them to bushranger hideouts, scattered in the wide and hostile country. The police force was quite inadequate to cover remote areas of bush as the distances were so vast. Later the police employed secret agents to try to whittle out such notorious bushrangers as Ned Kelly – a ploy that met with little success, due to lack of public co-operation and the bush telegraph. Nevertheless, Ned was eventually tracked down and captured by the police in a hotel at the small town of Glenrowan, forty miles north of Euroa.

assisted in the battle against the bushrangers. Corps of mounted troopers cooperated with the mounted police constables, who were reinforced with sworn-in special constables to hunt the

Mounted Australian police escorting prisoners for trial from country districts to metropolitan gaol in 1855. Pencil sketch by Samuel Thomas Gill. (State Library of New South Wales)

CHAPTER FIVE

PUNISHMENTS AND PRISONS

Throughout the centuries, governments have been expected to protect their citizens and property by controlling crime, enforcing the law and providing justice. Until the nineteenth century, the favoured deterrents were execution, transportation or corporal punishment, such as flogging, rather than expensive long-term imprisonment. The courts of criminal law were designed to incite terror in miscreants by imposing savage sentences and to offer sympathy to their victims. Before execution, prison clergy preached to convicted prisoners to fear God, urging them to confess their sins before they died.

In England and many European countries, there existed a multitude of fairly minor offences that were considered to warrant the sentence of death. By the end of the eighteenth century, English criminal law contained about 200 capital offences. Thus the penalty for stealing a small piece of lace, worth more than five shillings, was the same as for highway robbery and murder. For this reason, judges were encouraged to show mercy towards minor offenders and even to pardon some, or impose sentences of transportation to the various colonies, instead of hanging. Although death was the usual penalty for those convicted of highway robbery, transportation was substituted when violence had not been used. Despite this more humane policy, approximately 250 English highwaymen were still hanged in the twenty-year period between 1750 and 1770. Yet by the end of the century, fewer than one-third of those convicted of capital offences were actually hanged and many were transported instead.

TRANSPORTATION

Transportation to the colonies was the only practical option because few long-term prisons, other than for debtors, existed. Most convicts were transported from England to Virginia or Maryland, in America, to work in the plantations. Some became indentured or bonded servants and a few were sent to serve their sentences in Jamaica and Barbados. By 1770, about one thousand convicts a year were being transported to the British colonies. It proved good business for the ship-masters who carried them, who received, on landing, £10 to £25 for selling the convicts to the local landowners, the exact sum for each prisoner depending upon his age, fitness, length of sentence and any skill or trade he might possess. In addition, the Government paid a bounty of £5 for each convict landed. A few of the convicts later escaped from their new bonded colonial masters and took to the road, thus becoming the first of the early American highwaymen. Shipments of convicts continued until 1783, when Britain acknowledged American independence.

In 1788, after other potential destinations in Africa had been sought and dismissed as unsuitable, Port Jackson, about five miles to the north of Botany Bay in Australia, was selected as the alternative penal settlement. At first, the sailing ships deporting the convicts took seven or eight months to get there and the conditions aboard were appalling, with many dying of disease. Marine Corps officers on the ships were responsible for the discipline of the convicts, most of whom were locked up for the whole journey. Faster vessels later reduced the journey time to four months and the prisoners enjoyed better food and received better care from the ships' surgeons who were compulsorily present aboard. A few of those transported later returned to England when they had completed their sentence and took to the road again as highwaymen.

Many convicts awaiting transportation were kept in the hulks of ships which served as temporary prisons moored at Woolwich on the Thames and other estuaries. Hulks were also moored at Plymouth, Portsmouth, Chatham, Sheerness and even as far away as Gibraltar. The Government first took the decision to commission unseaworthy ships as prisons in 1776. The conditions aboard were so foul that some of the prisoners compared the experience to 'living in hell' and were even relieved to be eventually transported. However, a few served their complete sentences in the pestilence-ridden hulks and were released without even leaving the country; by day they were escorted ashore to perform hard labour in the naval dockyards or to work on river-bank improvements. Although transportation still took place to Australia until 1868, most of those with sentences of less than seven years were allowed to serve their time with hard labour in Britain, as some permanent long-term criminal prisons were established by that time.

In the early days the available prisons were primarily used for civil offenders, such as debtors, rather than criminals. Even in the early nineteenth century, the majority of prisoners in England were still debtors, held as a means of extorting from them the payment of the money they owed. One of the main prisons for debtors in London was the Fleet, which stood beside the Fleet river in Farringdon Street; it was demolished in 1840. Another was Marshalsea in Southwark, where Charles Dickens's father was imprisoned for debt in 1824; it was finally closed in 1842. There was also a separate debtors' prison at Newgate where prisoners with a little money bought themselves a relatively comfortable existence, including visits from relatives who brought in food. Occasionally the whole family lived with them and some went out to work to earn money. Felons, however, were held in another part of the prison at Newgate, shackled for a relatively short time before they were tried, usually convicted and taken away to be hanged or transported.

'BENEFIT OF CLERGY'

A few men escaped such punishments by claiming at their trial the 'benefit of clergy', first intro-duced in England in the twelfth century, during Henry II's reign. It entitled any ordained person to be tried solely by an ecclesiastical court instead of a secular one. If found guilty by the former, he would perhaps only serve a year's penance under the supervision of a bishop. Ecclesiastical courts could not inflict capital punishment. In medieval times, literacy was accepted as proof of ordination and this definition allowed many convicted felons, as well as the clergy, to escape the death penalty. Thus the better educated highwayman who came from a wealthy family would qualify. The system was abused because the accepted test for literacy in the seventeenth century was the ability to read, or recite, the first verse from Psalm 51 of the Bible. Many offenders learned the words by heart and recited the penitent's prayer:

> 'Have mercy on me, O God,
>   according to thy steadfast love;
>   according to thy abundant mercy
>   blot out my transgressions.
>   Wash me thoroughly from my iniquity,
>   and cleanse me from my sin.'

This became known as the 'neck verse', the means to saving one's neck. The privilege of claiming 'benefit of clergy' was drastically restricted in the sixteenth century during the Reformation but was not finally abolished until the early nineteenth century.

In France, as in England, there were few long-term prisons for criminals and in 1854 all prison building ceased completely. Hard-labour convicts were then transported to one of the French colonies, such as New Caledonia in the southwest Pacific, where conditions, too, were appalling. Earlier French prisoners were often sentenced to work as oarsmen in the galleys, and many Italian and Spanish criminals suffered a similar fate, although bandits were sometimes forced into military service instead, as happened in Genoa in 1755. This also occasionally occurred in England, when the offence was trivial and the men were considered young and fit enough to serve the colours.

METHODS OF EXECUTION

The early execution methods used throughout Europe were barbaric and staged in public. They were designed to inflict pain before death and at the same time to show the public that the authorities were in control. In Holland, for example, in the seventeenth century, the Amsterdam burgomasters, as representatives of the state, dressed in ceremonial robes for the execution and watched the proceedings, together with the magistrates, from the town hall windows. The execution method, here as in France and Germany, was breaking-at-the-wheel. The famous French bandit leader, Louis Mandrin, was executed in this way in 1755. In this procedure, the executioner first strapped the unfortunate prisoner across a large wheel, raised off the ground in a horizontal position. He then tortured the victim and broke his bones by beating him with an iron bar. This ensured a slow agonising death and the magistrates were empowered to decide how long the suffering of the condemned prisoner should continue, before the final death blows were delivered.

Equally barbaric was one of the execution methods used in England during the seventeenth century; this entailed the prisoner being hanged, drawn and quartered. One famous highwayman, Captain James Hind, was executed in this way on 24 September 1652. As a highwayman he mainly robbed the Roundheads, but because of his Royalist persuasions in the Civil War, he was indicted for high treason. Thus he was executed for this offence rather than for his many robberies on the road. The victim was first dragged to the place of execution on a hurdle. He was hanged for about six minutes and taken down from the gallows while still alive, then castrated, disembowelled and his intestines burned in front of him, before he was finally beheaded. The executioner, with axe and knife, next severed his torso, with limbs attached, into four parts. The head and body quarters were soaked in a preserving solution before being taken away to be displayed on prominent sites or gates, either on city walls or just outside them.

Deterrents were considered crucial and execution by hanging, drawing and quartering was especially dreaded, not merely because of the physical agony involved but also for a spiritual reason. A popular conception at the time was that to enter the afterlife it was essential for a man's body to remain whole; otherwise the soul would be destroyed. The same fear haunted many highwaymen in case, after hanging, their bodies were to be taken to an anatomy school for dissection. This was allowable under an Act of Parliament of 1752 which prescribed that a hanged murderer could be so treated in the cause of medical science. The surgeons were allocated ten bodies a year. This often proved too few which led to illegal disinterments and the growth of the profitable trade of body-snatching.

La Guillotine, also known as 'The Widow',
claimed the heads of highwaymen as well
as those of French aristocrats at the end of
the eighteenth century.

During most of the eighteenth century, hanging meant slowly strangling to death on the end of a rope. Not until 1783 was a trap-door drop designed from the scaffold, so that death became immediate as the prisoner's neck was broken by the hangman's knot. In Spain, capital punishment was also carried out by strangulation, but using the iron collar of the garrotte, attached to a post. The executioner placed the prisoner's neck in the collar, which was slowly tightened by a screw until asphyxiation occurred.

Scotland differed from England in the sixteenth and seventeenth centuries by using more widely an early form of guillotine, known as 'The

A Newgate inmate suffering 'peine forte et dure' to encourage him to confess guilt.

Maiden'. It was also used occasionally in England. Until 1650, the Yorkshire town of Halifax, for example, held such executions on market days so that more people could witness them. They were generally communal affairs, as all bystanders helped to pull the rope that raised the sharp blade over the victim's neck.

In 1792, Joseph Ignace Guillotin introduced a similar device for carrying out capital punishment during the French Revolution. The post of executioner in France was hereditary and the task was regularly passed from father to son for many generations. In France, the guillotine was not reserved only for suspected anti-revolutionists and aristocrats but for highwaymen and bandits as well. In fact, the first man to be executed after the machine was initially erected in the Place de Grève on 25 April 1792 was a highwayman, Nicolas Jacques Pelletier. It was originally called 'Louisette' before becoming known as 'La Guillotine', and later the French underworld nicknamed it 'The Widow'. In France, executions with the guillotine were held in public up to the beginning of the twentieth century. Its use was suspended in 1905, while a debate on capital punishment took place, but as no firm conclusions were reached, the guillotine was brought into service again in 1909 and continued to be employed until capital punishment was abolished in France in 1981.

NEWGATE PRISON AND TYBURN

In England, with so many highwaymen operating around the fringes of London, Newgate, as the largest short-term criminal prison in London, housed most of them before execution at Tyburn. The Tyburn gallows stood at Marble Arch to the west of present day Oxford Street, where it joins the Edgware and Bayswater Roads. A circular plaque set in the ground at a traffic island now commemorates the approximate spot. Tyburn lay well away from the City, its name originating from those of two streams that converged there, the Tye and the Bourne. The gallows was known as the 'Tyburn Tree' or 'Jack Ketch's Tree'. Jack Ketch, who served as hangman from 1663 to 1686, despatched over 200 rebel followers of the

Duke of Monmouth, following his attempt to overthrow James II. Thereafter his name was used generically to describe all hangmen.

Although Tyburn had been used for executions since the 1380s, the earliest permanent gallows was not erected there until 1571. This was built as an eighteen-foot-high tripod, with nine-foot-long crossbeams forming a triangle at the top, so that several men could be hanged from each crossbeam at the same time. Huge crowds witnessed the hangings and a large grandstand was erected in 1729, so that the gentry could obtain the best views. This spectator stand was called 'Mother Proctor's Pew', after its owner, who made a considerable fortune selling seats in it. Carts were also used as temporary viewing stands.

Not all condemned prisoners, however, made the journey to Tyburn. Sometimes the authorities erected portable gallows at the scene of the crime to make an example of a particular highwayman. During the trial proceedings prior to sentence, prisoners were usually brought to court in leg-irons. In Newgate, they were also frequently shackled to a floor or wall to prevent escape. While awaiting trial some were forced to confess their guilt or plea in the keeper's yard which later became known as 'Newgate's Press Yard'. Although designed as part of the keeper's residence, it was used to torture inmates by the method known as 'peine forte et dure'. Heavy weights were set on a board, which was then placed on the unfortunate prisoner's chest, after he had been spreadeagled and strapped down on the ground. The weights were increased until either a plea was obtained or the prisoner died with a crushed chest. Prisoners were also flogged at Newgate on the whipping blocks. The use of judicial torture declined as the eighteenth century progressed and 'peine forte et dure' was discontinued in 1772. Courts started to pay less attention to confessions and more to circumstantial evidence. This also happened throughout Europe but judicial torture was still used in France for some offences until 1788.

Newgate was a vast, forbidding, ill-lit and squalid place. Prisoners had little, if any bedding, other than the earthen floor and straw. Diseases,

such as typhus and typhoid, were rampant and this gaol fever killed nearly as many condemned prisoners as did the hangman. In addition, it killed gaolers, a few lawyers and even judges after they had visited the prison. Also, some prisoners committed suicide before their sentences could be carried out: those who died of gaol fever or committed suicide were buried in Newgate's own burial ground.

Constructed in the twelfth century, in the reign of Henry I, and later rebuilt several times, the prison's gatehouse originally formed one of the seven gates of the City of London, spanning Newgate Street. It was rebuilt in the fifteenth century, using money bequeathed by London's previous and most famous Lord Mayor, Dick Whittington, who died in 1423. One of the decorative features incorporated in the design was supposedly that of his cat. The Great Fire of London destroyed the building when it raged throughout the city on 3–4 September 1666. It was rebuilt during 1670–2 and new parts to the prison, designed by George Dance (the Younger), were added in 1770–8. In 1780, Gordon rioters, in their series of anti-Catholic demonstrations against property, attacked the building, freed the prisoners, some of whom were highwaymen, and then burned the interior. As a result, the incidence of highway robbery swiftly increased in London. The building was renovated and continued to be used as a prison until 1881; it was finally demolished in 1902. Five years later, King Edward VII opened a new building constructed on its former site. This was the Old Bailey Central Criminal Court.

Newgate Prison, when it incarcerated many highwaymen and other criminals, was divided into three quadrangles, one each for male and female felons and one for debtors. The building also incorporated the keeper's house, lodges for the turnkeys or gaolers, chapel, tap-room and the condemned cells. The turnkeys and visitors patronised the tap-room, although the occasional prisoner managed to secure a drink from it if he had money. As with debtors, money obtained favours for Newgate's felons, and some highwaymen, although shackled in the condemned cell, still

***The burning of Newgate Prison by Gordon rioters, in 1780, which set free
several highwaymen.***

managed to entertain visitors while awaiting execution. For example, many members of London's high society visited James MacLaine, a famous gentleman highwayman hanged in 1750. They included titled persons and members of the exclusive White's Club in St James's Street, where MacLaine formerly lodged.

At midnight before a hanging, the sexton rang a handbell brought from nearby St Sepulchre's Church to the archway of Newgate Prison, near the condemned cells. Twelve solemn tolls with double strokes announced that executions were to take place the following day, a summons to the condemned men and others to pray for their souls. The routine of ringing the bell at midnight was discontinued in 1783; instead it was rung on the morning of the executions, a practice that continued for the next hundred years. As Monday was the usual execution day, a service, attended by the paying public, was held during the Sunday evening for the condemned prisoners. The coffins destined to receive their bodies were visible from the pews. Many of the doomed men made a mockery of the service, ridiculing the chaplain to amuse their friends and putting on a show of bravado and defiance.

Newgate's stark prison gate.

spent his last few hours, in a broadsheet. This sold at a penny a sheet, on the execution day, to the crowds gathered at Tyburn and along the route to the gallows.

There were generally eight principal 'hanging-days' a year at Tyburn and these were made public holidays. As a result, the three-mile route to Tyburn along Holborn, St Giles and Oxford Street was lined with thousands of spectators. It was estimated that as many as 200,000 were present when Jack Sheppard, the famous felon, highwayman and notorious prison escaper, made the journey from Newgate to Tyburn in 1724. James

Some members of the prison clergy were not concerned entirely with the prisoners' spiritual welfare, but more interested in the money they could make if the prisoner was a well-known and notorious highwayman. Their privileged position gave them access to the condemned man and they used this time to gather as much information about him as possible. If they obtained an exclusive confession, so much the better. The chaplain then wrote and published the acquired life-story, together with an account of how the prisoner

Right: An execution scene at Tyburn held before a vast and chaotic crowd of spectators. Note the hangman calmly smoking his pipe on the triangular top of the gallows, while waiting for the condemned prisoner to arrive. Picture by Hogarth. (Guildhall Library, London)

MacLaine attracted about 100,000 spectators at his execution in 1750. The crowds especially cheered the highwaymen they admired, such as the popular John Rann, alias 'Sixteen-string Jack', who was hanged in 1774. Along the route, entertainers kept the waiting crowds amused and traders sold them gin and other refreshments. Pickpockets, too, did excellent business. The execution procession along the route took anything from about forty minutes to two hours, depending upon the size of the crowd. The occasion took on a carnival atmosphere and hanging days became known as 'Tyburn Fair' days.

On execution morning, the prisoners, after saying their farewells to relatives, were placed in carts for the journey; their coffins were loaded into the conveyances beside them. Before the condemned men entered the carts, a gaoler removed their irons and bound their arms, then placed a halter around their necks. The condemned were accompanied by the Sheriffs of London or their deputies, who led the procession with the chaplain reciting prayers.

Many prisoners washed, shaved and dressed in their best clothes for the occasion. The popular dandy 'Sixteen-string Jack' Rann wore a new pea-

green coat, with a huge nosegay in his button-hole. He also donned a hat with silver rings attached and wore a ruffled shirt. Another famous highwayman, Jerry Abershaw, put on a show of bravado at his execution in 1795 by dying with a rose between his teeth. Just before he was hanged, apparently recollecting that his mother had once warned him that he was bound to die with his boots on unless he gave up his criminal ways, he kicked off his footwear.

It became a custom to give nosegays of flowers to the condemned men at the gates of St Sepulchre's Church and also a last drink of ale or wine later at an inn along the route. Some highwaymen drank so greedily that they were quite intoxicated before the gallows was reached. The crowds heartily jeered prisoners who showed fear and did not behave with dignity. However, many remained sober enough to make a permitted farewell speech to the crowd, while the chaplain intoned prayers. Some related philosophically the cause of their downfall, others expressed their defiance of the law. A few even vented their anger by physically attacking the hangman, to the great amusement of the crowd.

Sometimes there were unexpected diversions. Now and then an emotional crowd would surge forward and attempt to hang the hangman; and a few instances occurred of a drunken hangman attempting to hang the chaplain instead of the prisoner! Some highwaymen kept talking for a long time, hoping for a last-minute reprieve that rarely materialised. Colonel James Turner, an ex-cavalry officer and friend of the diarist Samuel Pepys, was condemned for robbing a merchant in Lime Street, London of about £4500 in jewels and around £1000 in cash. Approximately 13,000 people attended the execution in January 1664 and Pepys himself, because of the large crowd, paid one shilling to obtain a view, standing uncomfortably on the wheel of a cart. Colonel Turner spoke for about an hour awaiting an expected reprieve, but it never came.

The law stipulated that after execution the prisoner must be buried in a woollen shroud. The condemned man had to pay for this, as well as the white cap placed over his face during the execu-

tion and the rope used to hang him. The hangman took the prisoner's clothes and kept them to sell later, if the condemned man could not pay. A few were hanged in their funeral shrouds, dressed ready to be placed in their coffins, thus saving the hangman the trouble of claiming their clothes after death. In the early days at Tyburn, the prisoner, after his farewell speech, was made to climb a ladder resting against the gallows. The noose was placed around his neck and the end tied to the crossbeam. He then had the option of jumping off the ladder or, if he declined, he was pushed off by the hangman.

Later a different procedure was adopted to simplify the task. After the rope was placed around the prisoner's neck, the horse-drawn cart, on which he stood, was driven smartly away and he was left to choke, dangling on the end of the rope. In order to hasten his death, relatives or friends sometimes pulled down on his legs, or paid the hangman to do this for them. The prisoner was

Left: A Tyburn execution in 1724. The prisoner, already clad in his funeral shroud, makes his farewell speech to the crowd.

Right: The former hangman's thatched cottage at Dorchester, Dorset which features in Thomas Hardy's story 'The Withered Arm'.

left hanging for about half an hour before he was taken down from the gallows. On a few occasions, the toes of the hanged person actually touched the floor or ground. This happened to the highwayman Robert Johnston when he was hanged at Edinburgh in 1818. He was suspended in agony until the crowd took pity on him, cut him down from the scaffold and carried him away. He was retrieved by the police after a skirmish, taken back, hanged and then took another forty minutes to die.

The hangman sometimes earned a little extra money by allowing ladies to mount the scaffold and touch the corpse; or he might permit them to do this in private after the execution. Many women believed that such an action would lead to a cure for disfigurements affecting their beauty. Rubbing the deceased's hand over warts, pimples and other blemishes was the most popular action, hopefully to ensure a magical cure. Thomas Hardy in his short story 'The Withered Arm',

from the *Wessex Tales*, described such a scene vividly, when Gertrude arranged with the hangman Davies for her to touch the neck of the hanged corpse, hoping this would cure the skin affliction on her arm.

The hangman also often sold pieces of the rope used for the execution because people believed it would charm away ague or fever when placed in contact with their body. In the early days, a poor-quality rope broke occasionally and the hanging procedure had to be started all over again, to the horror and dismay of the victim. The quality of the rope was later improved and a Bridport rope-making firm in Dorset supplied much of it, their product becoming known as the 'Bridport Dagger'.

GIBBETS

After an execution, relatives of the condemned usually claimed the body for burial, although some corpses were taken back for dissection to

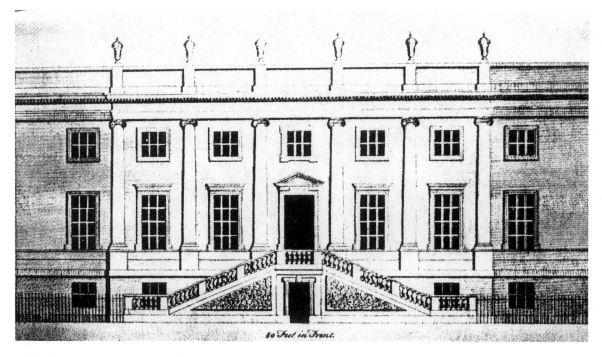

The 'Surgeons Theatre' situated at the Old Bailey, next to Newgate Prison. Highwaymen's corpses were dissected there for scientific study.

the 'Surgeons' Theatre', situated next to Newgate Prison. A few notorious highwaymen were also taken to roadside gibbets, erected at the scenes of their crimes. They were hung in iron frames and chains from the gibbet arms as deterrents to other would-be outlaws. Highwaymen and their relatives feared gibbeting because the bodies could not be buried in hallowed ground. As a preliminary, the corpse was coated in a preservative, such as tar, before being suspended from the gibbet for any passer-by to view. The gibbet was frequently located on a deserted common or a high prominent place where it would be conspicuous. Although executed criminals had been exhibited in this manner for many years, it was only officially legalised in 1752 to deter the robbery of the Royal Mail. At the end of the eighteenth century, the shooting of a Bow Street Runner by a highwayman also brought the penalty of hanging in chains. The body remained suspended for a very long time in its creaking rusty frame until it eventually rotted, presenting a most repulsive sight.

In order to deter relatives from removing the body, sharp spikes were driven into the post supporting the gibbet arm and sticky tar applied. This also dissuaded people who indulged in witchcraft and the preparation of bizarre medicinal cures from removing parts of the body for their rituals.

Although hanging on a gibbet took place after execution, there were occasions when a brutal and revengeful community performed the process before death. Such a case was John Whitfield, of Durham, who was gibbeted alive in 1777 at Wetheral, Cumbria. He was left to die in the misery of starvation but fortunately, after a few days, a passing mail-coachman took pity on him and put him out of his agony with a shot from his pistol.

It was not until 1834 that Parliament decided to abolish the practice of hanging executed criminals in chains. This was some fifty years after the ending of the degrading processions and public executions at Tyburn. Thereafter they were held outside Newgate Prison but still in public view.

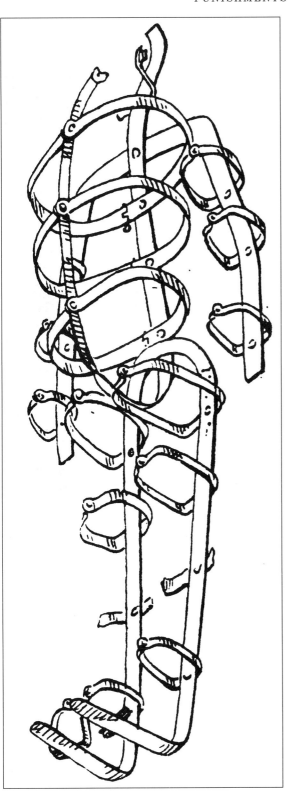

Highwayman Edward Miles was executed in 1791 and hung in chains on the Manchester road, near the Twystes, for robbery of the Royal Mail and the murder of a postboy.

The first executions carried out there were on 9 December 1783 when ten prisoners were hanged. Large crowds still attended but no grandstands were erected. However, the wealthy paid to hire rooms which overlooked the gallows and up to £25 was paid for window seats. Executions were not moved inside the prison, away from the public, until May, 1868, when the 'Capital Punishment Within Prison Act' came into force.

PRISON REFORM

The appalling conditions in prisons with their cruelty, punishments and lack of sanitation aroused thought in many minds of prison reform. At the end of the eighteenth century, John Howard, a philanthropist and high sheriff of Bedfordshire, led a vigorous campaign to improve conditions in English prisons after making local visits. He then investigated conditions at other prisons in England, Ireland and Europe. Howard favoured the payment of wages to the gaolers rather than the previous method of prisoners paying them fees for favours. An Act of Parliament of 1774 achieved this aim and prisons were gradually envisaged and used as a means of punishment, rather than merely a place to hold men awaiting trial or execution. In 1777, John Howard produced his momentous work on the 'State of Prisons in England and Wales' which gave some impetus to the campaign for prison reform. The main fundamental change suggested was the segregation of men from women in prisons and the provision of separate cells. Soon afterwards, in 1784, this was supported by an Act of Parliament. The end of transportation of convicts later encouraged further the idea of building new prisons. John Howard gave his name to the present-day Howard League for Penal Reform, founded in 1866.

Another early British prison reformer, Elizabeth Fry, a Quaker, visited Newgate Prison in 1813, with the aim of improving the appalling

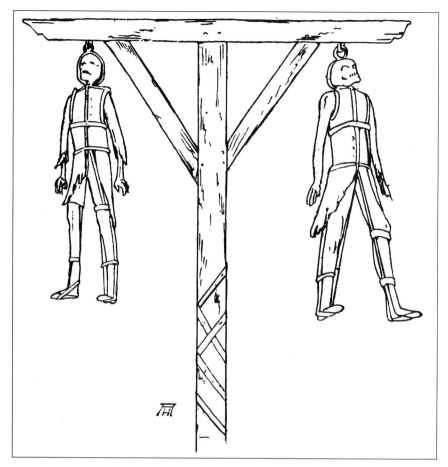

Left: A gibbet on Brandon Sands, 1785, with two bodies in chains. The metal cross-banding on the supporting post prevented relatives cutting down the gibbet.

Right: The whipping block at the Old Bailey.

conditions under which women were kept. She urged that women prisoners should not only be segregated from male felons but should also be supervised in light work by female prison officers. She also wanted them to be better clothed and fed. However, no really significant changes were possible without an expensive prison rebuilding programme. Later, she travelled throughout Europe in her quest to reform other prisons and expressed much concern on the lot of convicts transported to Australia.

The philosopher Jeremy Bentham suggested a new prison design called the 'panopticon' in which prisoners, housed in separate cells on several landings, could be watched from a central observation point. However, the development process was slow and it was not until 1842 that a large long-term prison, called Pentonville, was constructed in London. This design was based on the principle of solitary confinement. Pentonville later formed the model for other such institutions, built by central government throughout England to house large numbers of prisoners under tight security. In order to maintain discipline, prison officers meted out various legally approved forms of punishment. The treadmill was introduced to the English penal punishment system after its invention in 1817 by the British civil engineer, Sir William Cubitt. It consisted of a hollow cylinder, similar to a wide millwheel, with steps installed at intervals across the width of its circumference. The prisoners were forced to walk on the steps to turn the wheel for long spells of monotonous hard labour, and allowed only short rest periods during which they sat and watched other convicts doing the task. On occasions, the energy generated by the turning wheel was used to grind corn or to pump water.

Although in the course of the nineteenth century imprisonment gradually replaced corporal punishment, the courts retained the option of sentencing violent criminals to be flogged. Various types of lashes were employed, notably the feared cat-o'-nine-tails, consisting of nine knotted thongs attached to a handle. In the early days, whipping was brutally performed, with prisoners' backs being severely lacerated, salt sometimes being rubbed into the wounds to increase the pain.

In 1877, the Government took over the control of all prisons in England and Wales. Many had previously been privately owned and run purely for profit. Local gaols had been under the control of local authorities. A new body entitled the Prison Commission was formed to administer the whole prison system. Similar prison reforms took

The gallows outside Newgate in the Old Bailey. It was first used to hang ten prisoners in 1783.

place in America, Australia and continental Europe. In fact, it was the eighteenth-century Italian rationalist, Cesare Beccaria, who was one of the first to suggest the substitution of imprisonment for the death penalty as a form of punishment. In their early colonial days, nevertheless, both Australia and America inherited the English jurisprudence system, including 'benefit of clergy', but this privilege was generally abolished by the late eighteenth century.

In Australia, the convicts who misbehaved were disciplined mainly by flogging and later by solitary confinement or working on a tread-wheel when this punishment machine became available. Australian convicts worked in chains on the roads and other civil projects and were heavily guarded by the military. Following the experience of Britain with Pentonville Prison, each state in Australia began to build similar large prisons during the mid-nineteenth century. These housed some of the convicts still serving transportation sentences. As in England, capital punishment was carried out by hanging in Australia. In the early colonial days of the later eighteenth century, this often meant hanging the offender from a tree. Capital punishment continued to be per-

formed in public until 1853 in New South Wales and 1854 in Victoria.

In America, public hangings were also held, until they were abolished in New York in 1835 and in other states at various times later. In 1791, the first experimental long-term American prison was located in Walnut Street, Philadelphia, Pennsylvania. Unfortunately, it soon became overcrowded and therefore could not be used properly for its intended purpose. Further thought was given to the problem which eventually led to two improved alternative versions, known as the Pennsylvania prison system and the Auburn prison system. The former was based on a new type of building design, in which the central control room formed the hub, from which radiated rows of large identical prison cells built alongside corridors. The first penitentiary of this type was built during the early 1830s at Cherry Hill, Philadelphia. Each prisoner remained in solitary confinement and performed simple craft tasks each day in his cell. The prisoners never mixed together and met only the warders and the chaplain while serving their sentences. As the prisoners never came into contact with fel-

Australian convict chain gangs were employed in hard labour tasks, such as road building and harbour construction. They were closely guarded by the military. Picture from J. Backhouse's 'Narrative of a visit to the Australian Colonies'. London, 1843. (State Library of New South Wales)

In the American West, most captured outlaws were executed by hanging but occasionally they faced a firing squad. Photo engraving from 'Hands Up; or Thirty Five Years of Detective Life', by John W. Cook, Denver, 1897. (Library of Congress, LC-USZ62-2157)

low inmates, it was easier to maintain discipline. Although the cost of staffing such prisons was thereby reduced, the cost of building them was high. The economic factor thus prevented expansion of this type of system throughout America, although the prison design became popular in Europe.

The rival Auburn prison system, developed around the same time in New York, became more widespread and popular in most states. The prisoners were marched each day to a central prison yard to work beside one another and were forbidden to speak at all times. The work carried out was provided by contractors who set up workshops in the yard to utilise convict labour. Under this system, more prison staff were needed to instil the necessary discipline and impose the

strict rules of silence. However, the building design and lay-out were more economic than the Pennsylvania system. The outer walls of the fortress-like building enclosed rows of cells, built back-to-back in tiers.

In the United States, two main classes of prison subsequently developed – the federal penitentiary and the state penitentiary. The former incarcerated criminals who offended against the country's federal criminal code, the latter imprisoned those who offended against state laws.

Until the end of the nineteenth century, the purpose of long-term prisons in almost all countries was to impose retribution on prisoners for their crimes. It was not until the twentieth century that prisons attempted the additional tasks of correction and rehabilitation.

CHAPTER SIX

SEVENTEENTH-CENTURY ENGLISH HIGHWAYMEN

The predominant reason why English high-waymen, in comparison with footpads, murdered relatively few of their victims was that they operated on horseback and had the chance to escape. Also, the wearing of a mask ensured they were unlikely to be recognised later by their victims. During their robberies, high-waymen carried several pistols to protect them-selves and to terrify their victims, who usually offered little resistance. They took more than one weapon because of the notorious unreliability of the early flintlock pistols. Although shooting bat-tles with their victims were rare, they did occur, especially when armed guards or soldiers were present. As a rule, however, a greater danger to the life of a seventeenth-century highwayman was a treacherous accomplice or other informer who betrayed him. This happened increasingly after the passage of the Highwayman Act of 1693 which accepted the evidence of an accomplice and guaranteed his freedom from prosecution, pro-vided at least two of his confederates were con-victed.

The earliest recorded highwayman of the sev-enteenth century was a gentleman with the unusual name of Gamaliel Ratsey, who later acquired the even stranger nickname of 'Gamaliel Hobgoblin', as a result of the grotesque mask he wore when robbing his victims. Gamaliel was born in Market Deeping, Lincolnshire, the son of a wealthy gentleman. He left home to join the English army and served with distinction in Ire-land, under the command of the Earl of Sussex. Returning to Lincolnshire, he became bored with a quiet country life and took to the highways. He robbed with success, at first in the Spalding area of the county and then farther afield in East Anglia.

Ratsey was arrested and sentenced to be hanged for an earlier crime, but escaped from prison, wearing only his shirt. By chance he met two other highwaymen, and the trio carried out many daring robberies until the two confederates were captured. To save their lives, they informed on Gamaliel Ratsey, who was caught and hanged on 26 March 1605 in the town of Bedford.

Another early highwayman, born in 1603, was John Clavel, the son of a Dorset knight, Sir William Clavel, who lived in the manor of Smed-more. When John fell into debt he committed many highway robberies, especially at Gad's Hill and on the mail-coaches travelling along the Dover Road. He wore many different disguises during his hold-ups and paid several landlords of inns generously to shelter him. In 1626, despite all his skilful precautions, he was apprehended, convicted and sentenced to be hanged. He lodged an appeal with the King, and the sentence was commuted to imprisonment, after he had made a profuse apology.

Clavel was probably granted clemency because he was the eldest son of a knight. As few long-term prisons existed, he served his sentence in the King's Bench debtors' prison in London. While there, he wrote a treatise on highway law, the follies of committing crimes and hints for travellers on robbery avoidance, purely with the intent of lodging a further appeal and obtaining a pardon. He entitled his work *Recantation of an Ill-led Life* and his devious strategy brought the desired result, for he received a Royal Pardon, on condition he served in the army against France. However, Sir William never forgave his son and disinherited him. No more is known of John Clavel, although it was reported that he died in 1642.

Several early highwaymen dressed as women when they committed their robberies. Thomas Roland always adopted this form of disguise until he was executed in 1699. Another, Thomas Sympson, known as 'Old Mobb', only occasionally dressed as a female; it must have worked because he enjoyed an unusually long and successful period of several decades as a highwayman. He was born in Romsey, Hampshire and lived there for most of his life, mainly operating on the roads of southern England and the West Country.

'Old Mobb' invariably aimed high, concentrating on wealthy members of the aristocracy. Once he held up Sir Bartholomew Shower along the Honiton to Exeter road, in Devon. Unfortunately, the gentleman was carrying little money, which so infuriated 'Old Mobb' that he ordered the knight to write out a money demand note to his goldsmith in Exeter, for £150. He then bound his victim's hands and legs and bundled him under a hedge in a field, away from the road. Next, he cut the girth strap and bridle of the knight's horse and rode off to Exeter. The goldsmith, recognising Sir Bartholomew's handwriting, immediately honoured the demand note. Money in hand, 'Old Mobb' showed a benevolent side to his nature by riding back to his victim and releasing him from his bonds. Eventually, like so many before him, he ended his days at Tyburn, where he was hanged on 30 May 1691. He had a large family of five children and innumerable grandchildren, some of whom sorrowfully watched his execution. He made no speech or confession before he died.

LADY HIGHWAYMEN

Two women of the road who used the reverse disguise, dressing as men, were Mary Frith and Lady Caroline Ferrers. Mary Frith was probably born around 1584. Her father was a shoemaker and they lived in Aldersgate Street, near St Paul's Cathedral in London. Wild and aggressive from an early age, Mary later drank in taverns, carried a sword, smoked a long clay pipe and sometimes dressed as a man. She would also steal purses from passers-by, both inside and along the approaches to St Paul's Cathedral, using an accomplice who distracted the victims' attention

while Mary cut through the strings that secured the leather purses to their belts – a skill that earned her the nickname of 'Moll Cutpurse'. Mary was arrested several times, thanks to jealous informers, and she was branded four times on the hands as a thief.

'Moll' lived in Fleet Street for some years and at the age of fifty or thereabouts became a receiver of stolen goods from several gangs of thieves, often returning the ill-gotten property to their owners for reward. She was approaching sixty when she actually turned highwaywoman during the Civil War. She was an ardent Royalist and like many others, including her highwayman friend Captain James Hind, gained satisfaction by robbing Parliamentarians. Her most memo-

Mary Frith, purse-stealer, 'fence' and high-waywoman. Her criminal career in London spanned 50 years.

rable exploit involved General Sir Thomas Fairfax, a close ally of Oliver Cromwell. She held him up on Hounslow Heath and relieved him of a quantity of gold coins. During the incident, she shot the general in the arm and then killed two horses of his escort to prevent pursuit.

Shortly afterwards, the military captured her at Turnham Green when her horse went lame and she was sent to Newgate, tried and sentenced to death. However, she avoided her date with the hangman, apparently buying her pardon with a bribe of £2000, a huge sum in those days. (Other rich felons similarly escaped punishment, though £500 was usually enough, especially if murder had not been committed during the robbery.) Afterwards, 'Moll' continued her criminal life as a fence and eventually died, reputedly of dropsy, on 26 July 1659, when well into her seventies. She was buried in St Bride's churchyard, Fleet Street.

The other well-known highwaywoman, Lady Catherine Ferrers, came from an entirely different social background. She was born in 1662 and married Lord Ferrers at the age of sixteen. She performed her duties as lady of the house at Markyate, near Hemel Hempstead in Hertfordshire, but after several years became bored, eventually taking to the road, disguised as a highwayman. At night she ventured on the northern approach roads to London and, in order to leave the house undetected, used a secret passageway which led from her bedroom to the grounds of the large manor house. A steward observed her leaving the property one night. Although suspecting that she was the highwayman operating in the area, he never informed on her, not wishing to tarnish the reputation and good name of his employer, Lord Ferrers. Before he died, he told Lady Catherine of his knowledge and she suspended her night-time forays for a while. Later, she resumed and carried out several more daring highway robberies, until one night in 1684 her luck failed when she was wounded by a shot, during a hold-up of a coach. The exact circumstances of her death following the incident were never revealed, but it was thought she made her way back to her house whilst bleeding profusely. She managed to climb half-way up the stairs before collapsing and then died from her injury and loss of blood. She was twenty-two years old.

A few women turned to highway robbery to support their menfolk who were already involved in the crime. Sometimes the reverse occurred, as when highwaywoman Maud Merton came across her former lover Joseph Burton, better known as 'Daring Joe', begging on the streets after a life of gambling, lavish living and general dissipation. Maud persuaded him to take to the road with her as a highwayman but the joint venture later ended in disaster, with 'Daring Joe' being hanged at Tyburn.

ROYALIST HIGHWAYMEN

Captain James Hind, friend of 'Moll Cutpurse', was the only son of a saddler. He was born in 1616, at Chipping Norton, Oxfordshire, and received a sound education. He travelled to London on money borrowed from his mother and soon indulged in high living. He loved the company of ladies who much admired him for his politeness and wit. After turning highwayman, he would raise his hat when robbing them, and often refrained from taking all their valuables. He also occasionally gave money to the poor. When the Civil War broke out, he joined the Royalist army and fought at the battle of Worcester. He served with courage and later self-assumed the title of 'Captain'.

After the war, Hind joined forces with another highwayman, Thomas Allen, whom he had met before the war and they proceeded mainly to rob Parliamentarians. Once, they boldly attacked Oliver Cromwell's coach on its way to London from Huntingdon. The ambush ended in failure because the coach was well protected by seven guards. In the ensuing fight, Allen tumbled from his horse, being captured and later hanged at Tyburn. Captain Hind managed to escape with his life but only after riding his horse to exhaustion. He then led the life of a lone highwayman, concentrating on robberies where the potential rewards would be great and spending the money on lavish living. He never used violence if it could be avoided and only resorted to it when trapped.

Captain James Hind, a Royalist highwayman robbing Colonel Harrison, a Parliamentarian, in Maidenhead thicket.

After his eventual capture and execution in 1652 at Worcester by hanging, drawing and quartering, his head was placed on the Bridge Gate, spanning the River Severn, and his quarters stuck on other nearby gates. Later his head was secretly removed and buried within a week.

Another ardent Royalist highwayman was John Cottington, alias 'Mulled Sack', born in 1614, the son of a haberdasher. He started his early work-

ing life, when eight years old, as an apprentice to a chimney sweep. Later, in his early teens, he became a pickpocket, often frequenting one of Fleet Street's many taverns, where he drank sherry, a habit acquired from his father. His many successful highway robberies against the Parliamentarians included the stealing of a diamond-encrusted gold watch from Lady Fairfax, wife of General Thomas Fairfax; he later robbed

Royalist highway-man John Cotting-ton, alias 'Mulled Sack', robbing an army pay-wagon of £4000 at Shotover Hill, near Oxford.

the same lady again by removing the lynch-pin from her carriage when on her way to church, helped her to alight and at the same time relieved her of another watch. An attempted robbery of Oliver Cromwell himself, like that of Hind, ended, however, in failure. Cottington then teamed up with Thomas Cheney. The pair proceeded to rob Parliamentarians until one day disaster struck on Hounslow Heath, during an

attempted hold-up of a coach belonging to a high-ranking officer in Cromwell's army. A body of troops was following a short distance behind the coach and immediately gave chase. 'Mulled Sack' escaped but the unfortunate Thomas Cheney was wounded, arrested, tried and executed.

Shortly afterwards, Cottington formed a partnership with highwayman, Captain Thomas Horne. They attempted a further robbery of

Oliver Cromwell and his retinue on Hounslow Heath but with a similar result. Thomas Horne was captured, sentenced and hanged at Tyburn, while 'Mulled Sack' escaped yet again, resolving thereafter to work alone. His exploits amassed him a considerable fortune, which stood him in good stead when he was eventually arrested because he successfully corrupted the jury to secure his acquittal. Shortly afterwards, he killed a gentleman named Sir John Bridges, with whose wife he was conducting an affair, and fled to Germany. He later returned to England but was arrested and sent to Newgate Prison. He was tried, convicted and hanged in 1659 at the remarkably good age (for a highwayman) of forty-five. The execution took place at Smithfield Rounds, a site occasionally used instead of Tyburn.

William (or John) Nevison was another Royalist supporter. His real name was John Brace or John Bracey and he was born at Worley near Pontefract, Yorkshire in 1639, the son of a wealthy wool merchant. At an early age Nevison became a thief, even robbing his own family before stealing a horse from his schoolmaster and departing to London. Continuing his career of petty crime, he eventually stole £200 from his employer, a wealthy merchant, before fleeing to Holland, where he married a rich man's daughter. When her father discovered his son-in-law's true character and former thieving exploits in England, he reported him to the authorities. The deserted young wife reputedly died of grief. Nevison was imprisoned but managed to escape, fleeing to Flanders where he joined the army of the Duke of York, later to become James II, King of England, who had escaped to Holland after the defeat of his father, Charles I, in the Civil War.

William Nevison returned to England in 1659 when his regiment was disbanded, evidently taking to the road after the death of his father, who left him no money. His principal victims were Parliamentarians and occasionally moneylenders and bailiffs carrying rent money from farmers. As previously mentioned, he also levied a toll on northern drovers and carriers to ensure their safe passage.

Nevison earned the nickname 'Swift Nick' after a remarkable exploit in May 1676. Following a robbery at Gad's Hill, in Kent, at 4 a.m. he rode to the city of York, arriving at 7 p.m. on the same day. His route took him to Gravesend, over the River Thames by ferry to Tilbury, across the county of Essex, through Cambridge, on to Godmanchester and Huntingdon, and finally along the North Road for the final 120 miles to York.

The distance travelled was approximately 200 miles, taking about fifteen hours to complete. Given the average speed of between thirteen and fourteen miles per hour, including time for rests, there must be some doubt as to whether the same horse was used for the whole journey. Much later, for example, in 1831, in order to win a bet, the Regency squire George Osbaldeston changed horses twenty-eight times to ride a distance of 200 miles in eight hours and forty-two minutes. Likewise, in 1993, Peter Scudamore, the ex-champion National Hunt jockey, changed fresh thoroughbred mounts forty-eight times to beat George Osbaldeston's record time by just a few minutes. Although Nevison's journey took much longer and was over a similar distance, it seems unlikely that the feat could have been possible on a single horse.

After his arrival in York in the early evening, Nevison stabled his horse, changed into fresh clothes and set off for the bowling green where he knew the mayor was playing. In order to establish an alibi for his earlier crime, he walked over and asked the mayor the time; it was about 8 p.m. The ruse worked. A few weeks later, Nevison was arrested for the hold-up in Kent, but gained an acquittal at his trial by calling upon the mayor as witness to confirm he was in York on the day of the robbery.

Nobody in court thought it possible to complete such a journey in less than a day; and Charles II personally summoned the highwayman, who subsequently bragged of having fooled the law, to explain how he had achieved the feat. Nevison replied that he had ridden so furiously that the 'Old Nick', the Devil himself, could not have gone faster; whereupon the King dubbed him 'Swift Nick'.

The legendary ride from Kent to York in a single day by William Nevison ('Swift Nick'). The rest times and places were those suggested by the English novelist and journalist Daniel Defoe, in his 'Tour Through the Whole Island of Great Britain' in 1726.

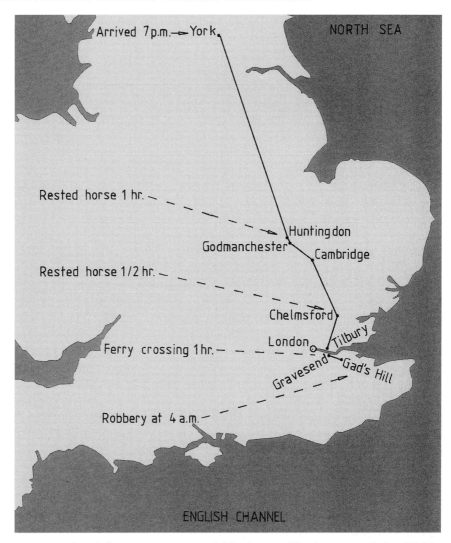

During the following century, the infamous highwayman Dick Turpin and his horse 'Black Bess' were fictitiously credited with the astonishing ride to York, actually accomplished by 'Swift Nick'.

Nevison proved he was a true master of deception after later being arrested for another crime of robbery and placed in Leicester Gaol. He pretended to be ill and arranged for a friend, claiming to be a physician, to visit him in prison. The bogus doctor painted a series of blue spots on Nevison's face and surreptitiously slipped him a sleeping draught; in due course the 'physician' called the gaoler and pronounced his patient dead of the plague. He arranged to take the body

away quickly in a coffin because of the highly infectious nature of the disease. Afterwards, Nevison awoke from his drugged sleep to continue his dashing life as a highwayman. He was arrested in 1676 for robbery and horse theft and upon conviction spent about five years as a prisoner in York Castle. Due for deportation to Tangier, to serve in the military there, he escaped once more. But his luck finally deserted him when he was betrayed by informers and arrested when visiting 'The Magpie' inn near Wakefield in Yorkshire. He was again taken to York Castle and put in chains until his trial at York Assizes. He was sentenced to death and executed on the Knavesmire on 15 March 1684 after making a farewell speech to the large assembled crowd. The following day he was buried at St Mary's Church, Castlegate, York.

'GENTLEMEN' HIGHWAYMEN

Isaac Atkinson's unusual speciality was robbing lawyers. He was born in 1614, the only son of a wealthy Berkshire landowner who provided him with a thorough education, including Oxford University. He never treated his studies seriously and led a degenerate life. His disappointed father removed him from Oxford to work on his estate, but Isaac ran away to London to mingle with low life. Desperate for money, he returned home to rob his father, who promptly disinherited him. Back in London, Isaac drifted deeper into crime and became a highwayman. After robbing Charles I's Attorney-General, Atkinson set his sights at lawyers. In a period of six months he stopped and robbed well over a hundred of them as they travelled around the country's law circuits.

He finally met his match when he changed his tactics to rob a lady near Turnham Green. When ordered to 'stand and deliver', she threw her purse over a hedge and galloped away on her mare. Isaac dismounted and walked over to retrieve the purse. Unfortunately for him, his horse was more interested in the lady's mare and galloped off in pursuit, catching up with her at Brentford in Middlesex. Realising what had happened, she raised the alarm and a party of men set off to the spot where the robbery had occurred. They found the stranded Isaac Atkinson in a nearby field but he fought fiercely to avoid arrest, killing four of the men and mortally wounding another. He was eventually overcome, tried and condemned to be hanged. In 1640, aged twenty-six, on the way to the gallows at Tyburn, he showed his contempt for the chaplain by stabbing him. Before he was hanged, he is said to have remarked philosophically: 'Gentlemen, there's nothing like a merry life and a short one!'

A highwayman who had an exceptionally long career of over forty years on the road was William Davis, born in 1627 in Wrexham, Wales. He married the daughter of a wealthy inn-keeper and it

is recorded they raised a large family of eighteen children. They successfully turned their hands to farming in the Bagshot region of Surrey and William took to the road in various disguises to supplement their income. He paid most of his debts in gold and so acquired the nickname of the 'Golden Farmer', reputedly keeping his criminal activities from the knowledge of his wife and family. Not even his neighbours suspected him over all these years. Davis mainly operated on Bagshot Heath but he also travelled and intercepted coaches as far afield as Salisbury Plain. His downfall eventually came when he attempted to rob a coach near London. He was wounded by a shot from a passenger, unmasked when he fell from his horse, and recognised. He was tried, convicted and hanged in 1690 at the age of sixty-four. Afterwards, the authorities hung his body in chains on Bagshot Heath.

One of the most famous English highwaymen of the seventeenth century was a Frenchman named Claude Duval, born in 1643 at Domfront in Normandy where his father worked as a miller. The village once had a strange reputation, for although the local parish priest baptised many children, he conducted few funerals. It seems most were executed at Rouen! Claude Duval left home when he was about fourteen years old and entered into service. At about seventeen, he was employed by the Duke of Richmond, an Englishman in exile, as a footman. After Charles II returned to the English throne in 1660, the duke, together with other Restoration exiles, including the Duke of Buckingham, returned to England. Duval, who accompanied the party soon succumbed to an expensive lifestyle of wining, dining and gaming. Inevitably he ran short of money, so he took to the road, his favourite hunting grounds being Hampstead Heath and the roads to the north of London.

Claude Duval gained the reputation of a gentleman highwayman by being impeccably polite to his victims, always raising his hat to ladies. According to Macaulay in his *History of England*, he demonstrated his manners in an incident near Hampstead Heath. Together with four companions, he stopped a coach containing a lady, her

William Davis, alias the 'Golden Farmer', holding up a tinker on a deserted heath.

husband and a servant, having received prior information that the gentleman was carrying £400. In order to prove she was not scared, the lady started to play a flageolet, whereupon Duval invited her to step down and dance with him. This she did, with her husband powerless to intervene. After the dance, Duval chivalrously handed the lady back into the coach and coolly asked her husband to pay a fee for the entertainment. When he handed over £100, Duval thanked him for his generosity and told him to keep the other £300. As a consequence, stories of the dashing young foreign highwayman quickly spread through the drawing-rooms of London.

On another occasion, Claude Duval and his confederates halted a coach on Blackheath, robbing a lady of most of her valuables, including a silver feeding bottle with which she was nursing her baby. The infant began to cry and the bottle was returned immediately. Later, briefly revisiting his native France, Duval continued to commit various crimes, including a confidence trick. He pretended he had realised the alchemist's dream of discovering a substance that could turn base metals into gold. He used the ruse to gain access to a rich merchant's house to rob him of his real gold.

Back in London, on an early January night in 1670 he carried out a hold-up that was to lead to his downfall. Celebrating his success too freely at the Hole-in-the-Wall tavern in Chandos Street,

Claude Duval robbing Squire Roper, Master of Buckhounds to King Charles II, in Windsor Forest.

Covent Garden, he was recognised as a 'wanted man' and although armed, he was too intoxicated to offer resistance. He was taken to Newgate Prison, later charged with six indictments and condemned to death. While awaiting execution, many ladies visited him in the condemned cell and a few of high rank pleaded with Charles II to pardon him. No pardon was granted and Claude Duval was hanged, aged twenty-seven, at Tyburn on Friday 21 January 1670. He declined to address the many sorrowful ladies who attended his execution, although the text of such a speech was later found on his body, in which he made many references to his high regard of the fair sex.

After execution, his admirers conveyed his body in a coach to the Tangier Tavern in St Giles-in-the-Fields, where he was laid in state. The room was draped in black and eight candles were lit around his bier, guarded silently by a group of men in black cloaks, while a host of people filed in and out to pay their last respects. The following day, Duval's coffin was taken to St Paul's Church, Covent Garden, the funeral being attended by a huge crowd, with many tearful lady mourners. He was buried under the central aisle of the church and an inscribed white marble stone was placed on top. Although no trace of the stone or inscription remained after the church was burned down in 1759, it was recorded that the epitaph read as follows:

Here lies Du Vall, reader, if male thou art,
   Look to thy purse; if female, to thy heart
Much havoc hath he made of both; for all
   Men he made stand, and women he made fall.
The second conqueror of the Norman race,
   Knights to his arms did yield, and ladies to
   his face
Old Tyburn's Glory, England's bravest thief,
   Du Vall, the Ladies' joy! Du Vall, the Ladies'
   grief.

Another gentleman-highwayman of repute was James Whitney, who promoted himself to the rank of 'Captain'. He was born in 1660 in Stevenage, Hertfordshire of poor parents, later working in a butcher's shop and then becoming landlord of an inn in his native county. Here he encountered many highwaymen who tried to persuade him to join their ranks. Tempted by the prospect of wealth and the lure of adventure, he eventually decided to try his luck, working both in groups and on his own. Because of his courage and intelligence, the 'Captain' was voted leader of his gang, which operated over a wide area, but insisted that no violence should be used during their robberies. Every so often he would disband them to deceive the authorities, then resume operations.

After an encounter with a party of dragoons sent out to suppress his band of highway robbers, Whitney was betrayed by a female acquaintance. He was captured, sent to Newgate and placed in heavy irons to prevent escape. Shortly afterwards, he was tried, convicted and sentenced to death. For his execution, he ordered from his tailor a new, richly embroidered suit, hat and peruke, worth £100, as he wished to die as a gentleman, but his gaoler refused to let him wear it. He tried to purchase a pardon but this was also refused and he was sent on the journey to the gallows at Tyburn. At the last moment, he was taken back to Newgate for additional questioning, as he had earlier indicated he possessed information on a Jacobite plot to kill the King. His story was not believed and he was hanged at the age of thirty-four on 19 December 1694 at Porter's Block, near Cowcross Street, Smithfield, instead of Tyburn.

SPORTING HIGHWAYMEN

Jack Bird from Stainford, in Lincolnshire, always appeared willing to accept a challenge and display a sporting instinct. At an early age he was apprenticed to a baker, ran away to join the army, promptly deserted and fled to Holland where he committed a robbery. He was arrested and the Amsterdam judiciary sentenced him to prison for one year with hard labour. Bird soon decided that prison duties were too hard and attempted to avoid them as much as possible. To cure him of his work shyness, the gaolers placed him in a deep tank and chained his ankle to the base. They then opened a series of taps, whereupon, to his alarm, water rushed in. Thoughtfully providing him with a hand-pump, they informed him they would return in an hour to observe whether he had pumped frantically enough to prevent himself drowning. Jack Bird survived the ordeal and was removed, exhausted, from the tank. Apparently he then settled down to serve his hard labour sentence.

Upon release he returned to England, stole a horse and became a highwayman. In one amusing incident, he held up a coach carrying an eccentric earl, his chaplain and two servants, a footman and a coachman. Bird demanded money and the earl offered to give him twenty guineas and suggested he fight him for it. Bird took up the challenge and the earl ordered his servants to stand aside. At the last moment, the chaplain offered to take the earl's place in the fight. Bird agreed, the fight commenced, and fifteen minutes later, he had won the match by knocking out the chaplain. When he volunteered to fight the earl as well, the latter declined, as whenever he boxed against his chaplain he was always well beaten, but rewarded Bird with the twenty guineas staked. After a succession of robberies, Jack Bird was eventually captured, convicted and hanged on 12 March 1690. Afterwards his body was taken to the Surgeons' Hall for anatomical studies.

Jonathan Simpson excelled at skating rather than boxing. Son of a wealthy merchant from Launceston, in Cornwall, he settled down happily as an apprentice draper in Bristol and was given money by his father to set up his own business. For a time things went well and he married a wealthy lady. Unfortunately she had been coerced into the match by her father, and after the wedding continued her liaison with the man she loved. Understandably vexed, Simpson left his wife and took to the road as a highwayman.

At first he was unsuccessful and he was apprehended for robbery, sent to Newgate Prison and sentenced to die at Tyburn. Just as the rope was placed around his neck, a reprieve arrived, purchased by his rich relatives. When taken back to prison, the gaolers allegedly refused to accept him. Having discharged him to be hanged, they were not allowed to admit him without a new warrant and he was released, upon which Simpson is said to have remarked: 'What an unhappy cast-off dog am I, that both Tyburn and Newgate should in one day refuse to entertain me!'

During one harsh winter in the 1680s, the River Thames froze near Kingston Bridge, west of London, and it was here that Simpson, spotting a couple of skaters, dismounted from his horse and joined them. He then tripped up his victims and robbed them as they lay sprawled on the ice, skating expertly away and escaping on his horse.

In a more conventional exploit, Simpson waylaid a gentleman who handed over a purse apparently full of coins. When he later opened it, he found he had been deceived because the contents were merely brass. A few months later, purely by chance, he encountered the same gentleman again in his coach. This time, Simpson took no chances and ordered the man to remove his trousers: the pockets contained not only money but also a gold watch and snuff-box. During his final robbery, however, his horse was shot from under him and he fell wounded. Simpson was captured, tried, found guilty and hanged at Tyburn on 8 September 1686.

RELIGIOUS HIGHWAYMEN

A highwayman who turned from religion to crime was Jacob Halsey. He was born in Bedford of very wealthy parents, who were farmers, and brought up by them in the Quaker faith. He was often moved to speak at meetings, declaring that he had visions and that a voice sometimes commanded him to do strange things. One of the congregation, as a joke, stood below his bedroom late at night, shouted for Jacob to wake up and commanded him to go to the church and smash all the windows. Halsey apparently obeyed the voice and was arrested the next morning. For his misdemeanour, he was placed in Bedford Gaol where he mixed with many unsavoury characters. Upon release, he encountered so much local ridicule that he left the area and after a spate of petty thieving took to the road as a highwayman, operating mainly in the southern counties of England.

Halsey worked alone, wearing many different disguises, and reputedly often addressed his robbery victims in biblical terms. Although initially polite, he soon turned vicious when thwarted. He was violent both to men and women, although he claimed in his execution speech that he had never murdered anyone. He was finally apprehended when attempting to rob the Earl of Westmorland, near his estate at Wateringbury in Kent. He was sent to Maidstone Gaol and was executed there in April 1691.

EIGHTEENTH-CENTURY ENGLISH HIGHWAYMEN

Violence on the highways was more common in eighteenth-century England than it had been before and after the Civil War when the so-called gentlemen highwaymen were out and about. There were, nevertheless, exceptions, as exemplified by the few well-educated sons of clergymen who took to the road, short of funds and unable to maintain the high standard of living to which they had become accustomed at home with their parents.

CLERGYMEN'S SONS

One such individual was Nicholas Horner, the son of a Devonshire minister from Honiton. His first robbery attempt failed miserably and he was apprehended. His father's influence saved him from the death penalty and he was sentenced instead to seven years' transportation. Having learned nothing from the experience, Horner returned home and resumed his criminal career. Again he was captured but this time the authorities showed him no mercy. He was hanged at Exeter in 1719.

A very similar case was that of minister's son Thomas Barkwirth. He was educated as a classical scholar and also excelled in French and Italian. His first highway robbery on Hounslow

'Gentleman' highwayman James Maclaine's most famous victim was English writer Horace Walpole. Maclaine became a very popular figure with the ladies.

Heath gained him the sum of just twenty shillings. He had little time to spend it, as he was captured one hour after the theft and hanged in December 1739.

A clergyman's son who enjoyed a much longer and successful career as a highwayman was James Maclaine. He was born in 1724 in Ireland, the son of a Scottish Presbyterian minister, who gave him a sound education and planned for him to become a partner with a Scottish merchant in Rotterdam. When Maclaine was eighteen years old, his father died but he left him a moderate fortune. Unfortunately, the lad squandered the inheritance in Dublin in less than a year. As a consequence, he took the job of a gentleman's butler but was dismissed by his employer for dishonesty, during a visit to London.

Maclaine remained in London and borrowed money to clothe himself in elegant fashion, resolving to marry a rich heiress. A wealthy horse-dealer's daughter did indeed become his bride and they opened a grocer's shop in London with her dowry of £500. All went well until his wife died in 1748 of smallpox. Deeply distressed, Maclaine arranged for his wife's parents to look after their two young daughters and sold the business. But he soon squandered the

The trial at the Old Bailey in 1750 of highwayman James Maclaine. Many of London's high society were present.

money that remained after the settlement for his daughters, and took to a life of crime on the road.

Maclaine went into partnership as a highwayman with a neighbour, William Plunkett, who had lost his money when his apothecary business failed. At first, Plunkett instigated and took the major role in their highway robberies but Maclaine later overcame his initial nervousness and earned the nickname of 'The Gentleman Highwayman', partly because of his politeness and partly his elegant clothes and the fine Venetian mask he donned during his hold-ups. In the intervals both men led the lives of gentlemen of leisure, residing in St James's, London, Maclaine posing as an Irish squire and having a second lodging in rural Chelsea. He still cherished hopes of wedding a rich heiress and giving up his criminal career.

The highway robbery which made Maclaine famous involved the famous man of letters Horace Walpole, son of Sir Robert Walpole, regarded as Britain's first Prime Minister. He and Plunkett, intercepted Walpole's carriage in Hyde Park, when he was returning home one night in November 1749. During the ambush, Maclaine accidentally fired his pistol and the shot grazed Walpole's face before hitting the carriage roof. He later expressed his regret at the unfortunate incident by writing two letters to Walpole apologising for his bad behaviour and even offering to return the stolen articles in return for a small fee. Walpole never replied, although he informed many people in London of the incident.

Maclaine travelled to Holland to stay briefly with his brother Archibald, a pastor in The Hague, then returned to London to resume his partnership with Plunkett. Their careers ended when they committed two robberies on a fateful day in June 1750. In the early morning they held up the Salisbury stage-coach near Turnham Green and, later in the day, Lord Eglinton's carriage on Hounslow Heath. The haul from the first robbery included a lace waistcoat and, from the second, Lord Eglinton's blunderbuss, his portmanteau and fifty guineas. Later Maclaine attempted to sell some of the stolen property, including the lace from the waistcoat. A lace-maker recognised it from the description advertised and circulated after the theft. Maclaine was captured and vainly tried to place the blame on Plunkett, who promptly vanished. Maclaine stood trial and was found guilty.

The trial caused much discussion among London's high society because he had become a popular and well-known figure, especially with the ladies. In fact, Horace Walpole recorded that on the Sunday after the trial about 3000 people visited him in the condemned cell at Newgate Prison, many fainting in the crush, including the prisoner himself. Walpole expressed his sorrow for Maclaine's plight, recalling the earlier polite correspondence, but could do nothing to help. Maclaine was executed on 3 October 1750 at Tyburn. The hanging attracted a high percentage of ladies among an estimated 100,000 spectators.

One or two eighteenth-century highwaymen actually performed some good deeds. For example, in the early 1720s Benjamin Child used ill-gotten gains to buy freedom for some of the debtors in Salisbury Gaol. Shortly afterwards, Jonathan Wild, the 'Thief-taker General', captured this benevolent highwayman who was later executed and his body hung in chains on Hounslow Heath. Two other highwaymen, 'Captain' Evan Evans and his younger brother once managed to perform a dubious good deed and a robbery at the same time when they encountered a press-gang, escorting twenty roped, bedraggled men to Portsmouth. The Evans brothers ambushed the convoy, set the captive men free and robbed the constables. Later the authorities apprehended the brothers and showed them no mercy; both were hanged in 1708.

Wealth or a high position in society, as always, often brought mercy. Sir Simon Clarke, a baronet convicted of highway robbery in Hampshire, together with his confederate, Lieutenant Arnott, were sentenced to death at Winchester Assizes in 1731, despite a moving speech made at the trial by the baronet. Afterwards, Clarke's influential friends managed to get the supreme penalty laid aside for him but not for his accomplice. The appeal to the King was launched on the grounds that the baronet's ancestors had performed outstanding services to both king and country.

Earlier in the century no such plea could possibly be made for Jack Ovet, who came from humbler stock. This highwayman was an expert swordsman and on one occasion held up a squire who taunted him that he was a coward hiding behind his pistols. Ovet later related that after the squire challenged him to a duel with swords he put away his pistols and dismounted; the ensuing fight ended with Ovet running his sword through his opponent and mortally wounding him. The sporting highwayman was later captured and hanged in 1708.

John Hawkins was a butler before turning into a high-stakes gambler, which led him to take to the road to finance his losses. He was born in Staines, Middlesex and was forced to leave his job in service after his employer suspected him of robbery. Without references, and unable to gain another job in household service, Hawkins became a highwayman and concentrated on robbing the aristocracy around London and mail-coaches in other parts of England, on one occasion holding up the Bristol Mail at Colnbrook. At first he worked alone but later with several accomplices. One of these was the landlord and livery keeper of a tavern at London Wall. He supplied the horses with which Hawkins carried out his robberies. However, he usually lost his ill-gotten gains immediately at the London gaming tables, which he visited two or three times a week. Occasionally he travelled to Amsterdam in order to sell stolen jewels. Jonathan Wild made many attempts to apprehend him but only succeeded in taking some of his accomplices. On 21 May 1722, however, betrayed by his confederates, Hawkins met the hangman at Tyburn; after execution, his body was hung in chains on Hounslow Heath.

JACK SHEPPARD

At about the same time, John (Jack) Sheppard, who indulged in all forms of crime, achieved notoriety as a master escaper from prisons. Often referred to as a highwayman, no court records exist to prove he actually was one, although this was probably due to the fact he was never caught for such an offence. This eighteenth-century 'Houdini' was born in December 1702 at Spitalfields, London, the son of a carpenter. His father died when he was a young boy and his mother brought him up in Bishopsgate Workhouse. He followed in his father's trade but ran away from his apprenticeship and was arrested for this offence in 1723, then turning to thievery, pickpocketing and housebreaking, and often working with a criminal accomplice, Joseph Blake, known as 'Blueskin'.

Sheppard became a frequent customer at the 'Black Horse' alehouse in Drury Lane where he drank heavily. He had several mistresses, his favourite being Elizabeth Lyon, nicknamed 'Edgeworth Bess'. It was said that these women encouraged him in his criminal activities.

Sheppard obtained his first experience of prison when committed to St Giles's Roundhouse in London for housebreaking in April 1724. A slender, agile man, he escaped by breaking out through the roof. The next month he was again arrested for pickpocketing and this time was sent to Newgate Prison, where by chance he met his mistress Elizabeth Lyon, an inmate for a similar offence. The gaoler put them in the same cell in the belief they were man and wife. Friends visited them in prison and smuggled a tool to Sheppard which he used to file through his fetters. Watched by 'Edgeworth Bess', he chipped away at the masonry around one of the bars in their cell window, until he managed to remove it. In order to escape they still had to negotiate a twenty-five-foot drop to the yard below; this was achieved by tying together a blanket and sheet and securing it to a remaining cell window bar. Having reached the yard, Sheppard and his mistress faced a twenty-

two-foot-high prison wall. They decided instead to clamber over the prison gate, using the locks and bolts as footholds.

After their escape, they separated and Jack left briefly for the country, where he may have operated as a highwayman. However, he soon returned to his old criminal haunts in London. He committed housebreaking with accomplices and injured one in a quarrel over the distribution of the spoils. He also gained the enmity of Jonathan Wild, whose protection he refused. As a result, Sheppard was arrested and sentenced to death at the Old Bailey. He was sent back to Newgate and locked in a condemned cell with a solid door, over the top of which was a small

Jack Sheppard's escape from Newgate Prison in August 1724, ably assisted by his mistress 'Edgeworth Bess' and Poll Maggot.

opening guarded by iron spikes. But security, as always, was very lax. A visiting lady friend managed to pass him a tool through the gap in the door, and with this Sheppard filed and sawed through one of the spikes. When a group of ladies, including 'Edgeworth Bess' next visited, he bent the spike aside, pushed his head and shoulders through the gap and was pulled out by his friends while the turnkeys were busy drinking elsewhere. It was rumoured that he even had time to don female dress. In any event, Sheppard and his female accomplices quietly walked out and escaped in a hackney carriage.

Shortly afterwards, Sheppard was again apprehended when boldly strolling across Finchley Common on 10 September 1724. Back he went to Newgate, this time being held in the most secure cell available. In addition, the gaolers manacled his hands and put his legs in irons which were stapled to the stone floor. His fame as an ingenious prison escaper brought him many visitors but this time no smuggled tools. One night, how-

Jack Sheppard's escape route from Newgate Prison on 15 October 1724.

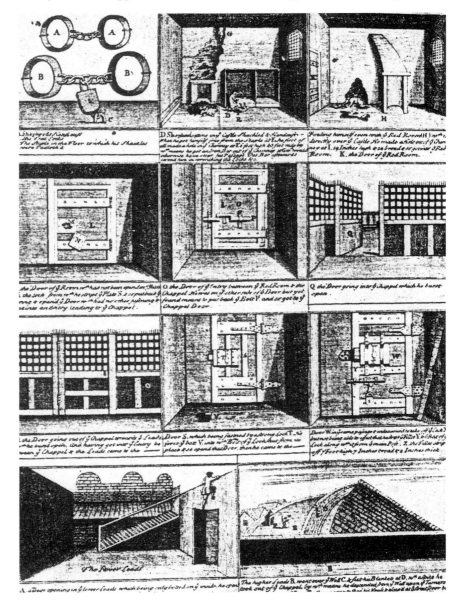

Jack Sheppard locked in special irons to prevent a further escape from Newgate Prison.

ever, after the gaolers had checked his irons, Sheppard tried to get rid of his handcuffs. Nobody knows exactly how he succeeded. One theory was that he held the connecting chain in his teeth and stretched and squeezed his fingers together until he managed to slip his hands free. Then, apparently, he found a bent nail which he used to pick the padlock that secured his irons to the floor. Another theory claimed that he forced apart the weakest link in the chain that tethered his legs. Once free, he wrapped a severed length of chain around each of his legs, holding them in place with his garters, so that they would not hamper him.

He attempted to escape through the chimney but found a metal bar across it. After considerable effort, he freed the obstructing bar and used it to knock a hole higher in the chimney wall to escape into the room above, which was rarely used. He forced the lock of the door and found himself in a passageway that led to the chapel. The entrance door was bolted on the other side. Sheppard proceeded to knock holes with his bar in the masonry beside the door, until he could put his hand through and draw the bolt.

It was later discovered that he had forced open four more doors in this deserted part of the gaol to reach an opening that overlooked the prison wall. He used a blanket brought from his cell to lower himself over the wall and land on the roof of an adjoining house. He stayed there for a while and then entered the house through a garret window, before escaping to the street below. Having difficulty in removing the chains still fastened around his legs, he hid for a time until he managed to knock off his fetters with a convenient stone or tool.

Within a short space of time he committed other robberies, including that of a pawnbroker in Drury Lane whom he robbed of a suit, a snuffbox and a sword. The funds enabled him to start drinking heavily again. Once he was recognised by a boy who informed the authorities. Sheppard knew little of his arrest because he was hopelessly drunk at the time. He was sent to Newgate Prison yet again and the previous sentence of execution stood after his identity had been confirmed. This time the turnkeys took no chances, watching him constantly, day and night, and charging a profitable fee to his many visitors. While awaiting execution, Sheppard sat for the royal portrait painter, Sir James Thornhill.

Sheppard still hoped to escape again and reportedly obtained a penknife with which he intended to cut the bonds from his hands when on the execution cart, jump down and get lost among the friendly crowd. However, the penknife was discovered and removed, and his hands placed in iron cuffs. As a last resort, it was rumoured, he paid friends to take his body away as quickly as possible after the hanging, hoping they would still be able to revive him, a clear impossibility, due to the tumultuous crowd, estimated at 200,000, present. On 16 November 1724 he was hanged at Tyburn, still not quite twenty-two years old. During riotous scenes and commotion, his friends eventually took the body to a tavern, the 'Barley Mow' in Long Acre, where it stayed overnight. The following day, Jack Sheppard was buried in the churchyard of St Martin's-in-the-Fields.

DICK TURPIN

Jack Sheppard gained his fame by his daringly ingenious escapes but England's best-known highwayman, Richard (Dick) Turpin, gained his renown, a century after his death, through the publication of a fictional and glamorised version of his life, contained in *Rookwood* (1834), a novel by the romantic historical writer William Harrison Ainsworth. In reality, Turpin was a cruel, sadistic and ruthless highwayman. He was born on the 21 September 1705 in the village of Hempstead, seven miles from Saffron Walden, Essex, where his father kept an alehouse, then called the 'Bell Inn' but now the 'Rose and Crown'. Turpin

learned to read and write under the tuition of the local schoolmaster, John Smith, who later was to play a major role in his downfall.

After leaving school, Turpin was apprenticed, at the age of sixteen, to a Whitechapel butcher. Later he married and eventually in 1728 owned his own butcher's shop in Thaxted, Essex. He embarked on a career of crime by stealing cattle and sheep to sell in his shop. When the offence was discovered, Turpin ran away and joined a notorious gang of smugglers who were operating on the Essex marshes near Canvey Island. In due course, he even started to rob his partners of their share of the spoils and was forced to flee to escape their wrath.

He joined a gang of deer poachers in Epping Forest and his skill in the butchery trade proved an asset in the disposal of carcasses. They smuggled the venison into the London market by concealing it beneath cartloads of vegetables. After a while, he drifted into housebreaking, initially as a

***Dick Turpin clearing Hornsey toll-gate in London to escape from the law.
Tops of toll-gates were spiked to discourage horsemen from attempting to jump them.
(Guildhall Library, London)***

member of a gang, led by a rogue named Gregory. They robbed over a large area of the counties neighbouring London – Essex, Middlesex, Surrey and Kent. The gang brutalised many members of the households they chose to rob. On at least two occasions, Turpin forced servants to disclose where their employers' valuables were kept by callously holding them over the household fire. Rewards of up to £100 were offered for the capture of gang members and this soon put informers on their trail. They were traced to one of their favourite haunts, a tavern in Westminster. After a struggle, most of the villains were arrested but Turpin escaped, together with another felon named Rowden. The leader of the gang, Gregory, was executed and hung from a gibbet.

Turpin hid for a while and his wife brought him food. Then, in conjunction with Rowden, he turned highwayman, operating mainly on Putney Heath, Barnes Common and Blackheath. Later he joined forces with another highwayman, Tom King. They carried out innumerable robberies of lone travellers and stage-coaches on the Essex roads and on the London to Cambridge road. In order to evade pursuit and capture they retreated afterwards to a hide-out they built in the depths of Epping Forest and were brought food by Turpin's loyal wife.

On one occasion, a forest-keeper's servant, Thomas Morris, came across the hide-out and Turpin shot him dead. A 'Wanted for Murder' notice was immediately circulated, describing Turpin as about five feet nine inches tall, about thirty years of age, of brown complexion, with broad shoulders, prominent cheekbones and a face badly scarred with smallpox. Earlier eye-witnesses reported he often wore a gold-lace-trimmed hat during his robberies. Soon after the shooting, Turpin and King were intercepted near a tavern in Whitechapel; a coachman had recognised a stolen horse ridden by one of them and they were followed to the inn. An arrest was attempted and during the mêlée Turpin accidentally shot King, who was captured, and galloped away on his horse.

To avoid arrest, Turpin left Essex for Lincolnshire. He stayed briefly at Long Sutton where he narrowly escaped capture for sheep- and horse-stealing. He then departed to Yorkshire where he started a business as a horse dealer under the assumed name of John Palmer. A year later, in October 1738, he was arrested, being held initially on a charge of stealing a game-bird and later for horse theft. While imprisoned in York Castle, pending his trial, he wrote, under his pseudonym 'John Palmer' to his brother-in-law, who lived in Hempstead, Essex, asking for help, such as a reference. Unfortunately for Turpin, the letter was shown by coincidence to John Smith, his former schoolmaster who also still resided in Hempstead. He immediately recognised the handwriting and informed the magistrates, perhaps influenced by the special £200 reward on offer for the capture of his notorious former pupil. He then departed to York to identify Turpin, whose fate was sealed at York Assizes on 22 March 1739. Turpin calmly accepted the inevitable hanging sentence.

While awaiting execution, Turpin received many visitors. He also made elaborate plans for the impending final event by ordering a new fustian suit and a pair of shoes to wear at the gallows. He also hired five men, paying them three pounds ten shillings, to follow the execution cart as mourners and wear black gloves and black mourning bands on their hats. It was reported that Turpin behaved with dignity on the day. On the way to the gallows on the Knavesmire, just outside the town walls of York, he raised his hat to the ladies and waved to the crowd, although people close by observed that his right leg was trembling. At the scaffold he chatted to the hangman for a considerable time until the crowd became restless. His life ended, at the age of thirty-three years, on Saturday, 7 April 1739, when with a heroic flourish he flung himself from the gallows, attempting to break his neck with the hangman's rope rather than suffer a lingering death just dangling on the end of it.

After the execution his body was brought back to the 'Blue Boar' inn at Castlegate and the following morning he was buried in St George's churchyard, York. Shortly afterwards, mourners surprised some body-snatchers who had just finished illicitly disinterring the corpse for dissection. They gave chase and later found the corpse abandoned in a doctor's garden. They carried the body back to the graveyard for reburial but first filled the coffin with quicklime to prevent a recurrence.

WILLIAM PARSONS

William Parsons never gained the fame of Dick Turpin, despite operating as a highwayman in both America and England. Born in 1717, the youngest son of a Nottinghamshire baronet, Parsons was given a privileged education at Eton. But he spent much time playing cards, and was expelled for stealing money to pay off his gambling debts. His exasperated father arranged for him to join the Royal Navy as a midshipman and he set sail for the West Indies on his first voyage. Later, he was dismissed from the service for cheating at cards, an unforgivable offence for a young officer. His friends deserted him when he arrived back in England and soon he was almost destitute. He had expectations of his aunt, the Duchess of

Highwayman William Parsons robbed both in America and England. He was executed in 1751.

Northumberland, leaving him an inheritance, but she changed her will and his dream was shattered.

His father attempted to help him by obtaining a post with the Royal Africa Company in Gambia, but Parsons was soon on his way home after a dispute with the governor. His long-suffering father encouraged him to join the Life Guards but did not offer the £70 required to buy him a commission. William then misappropriated funds belonging to his brother, who had received a legacy from their aunt, using the money to dress elegantly and mixing in the right social circle to wed a young lady of considerable wealth. He lived extravagantly for a while, with a house in a fashionable area, servants and a private carriage. A commission was also purchased for him to join a foot-regiment in the army. But his mania for gambling continued and he lost heavily, squandering his wife's fortune. In the end, he had to sell his commission to pay some of his debts.

In order to evade other creditors, Parsons went into hiding and indulged in a series of crimes, including forgery and fraud. By a confidence trick, he also stole valuable rings from a jeweller and uniforms from a tailor. He was finally apprehended when forging a warrant to obtain money, tried at Maidstone Assizes in 1745, convicted and sentenced to transportation to Virginia, to work in the plantations.

Parsons's wealthy employer took pity on the apparently well-educated young man whom he saw each day toiling in the sun, and after several weeks befriended him, inviting him to his house. When a suitable opportunity arose, Parsons repaid the gentleman's kindness by stealing one of his best horses. He took to the road and became one of the earliest highwaymen in America. Soon he accumulated enough money to pay his passage back to England.

He landed at Whitehaven, Cumberland (now part of Cumbria). Here he obtained money under false pretences to pay his stage-coach fare to London. On arrival, he took lodgings near Hyde Park, hired a horse and committed a highway robbery on Hounslow Heath. Parsons continued to work alone as a highwayman – his favourite sites were Turnham Green, Kensington and other deserted spots to the west of London – and, perhaps out of bravado, never wore a mask. As soon as he acquired a large sum of money, he swiftly lost it at the gaming tables and so the vicious circle continued. On one occasion, he set out to rob a servant who was carrying a large sum of money for his master. This was to prove Parsons's final day of freedom. He was recognised on his way to intercept the servant, by a previous victim he had robbed, who followed him to Hounslow Town. There he denounced Parsons who was captured without resistance and his pistols taken from him. The landlord of the 'Rose and Crown' inn confirmed the identification and others also easily recognised the highwayman who never wore a mask. Sent to Newgate Prison, he was also charged with violating and returning from his previous transportation sentence. His wealthy father and his loyal wife tried their utmost to gain a pardon but it was to no avail. Aged thirty-four, he was convicted and hanged at Tyburn on 11 February 1751.

WILLIAM PAGE

A highwayman who showed extraordinary ingenuity and meticulously planned all his robberies was William Page. He was born in 1730, the son of a working-class family who lived at Hampton, to the west of London. His father died at an early age and his mother brought him up and arranged an apprenticeship for him with a relative, a haberdasher in London. William became interested in fashionable clothes and the need for money to purchase them eventually led him to rob his employer. He was dismissed rather than reported to the authorities, no doubt due to the family connection. Although he lacked references, he managed to obtain a job as a footman to a gentleman. One day, travelling with his master in his carriage, they were ambushed by a highwayman. Page marvelled at the large sum of money acquired by the masked rider within a few minutes and apparently resolved there and then to try his own fortune on the road. He secured a

horse and pistols and committed several robberies in quick succession at Highgate Hill, to the north of London, and near Hampton Court, to the west. He also held up the Canterbury stage-coach at Shooter's Hill, on the London to Kent road.

Page realised that his early successes had largely been due to luck and decided to plan in detail his future robberies. This cautious approach led him to suspend his criminal operations for a while and he took lodgings in Lincoln's Inn Fields, posing as a law student. He mixed with fashionable society, travelled and drew detailed maps of all the main and minor roads, within a twenty-mile radius of London, noting the safest ambush points, one of which was Putney Heath.

Resuming his criminal ways, he decided to allay suspicion by dressing as a gentleman and driving a phaeton and pair to a deserted spot close to his chosen ambush place. On arrival, he changed into old clothes, put on a disguise with a black wig and saddled up one of the carriage horses. After the robbery he returned to his phaeton, changed back into his fashionable clothes and drove back to London.

His plan for one such foray went badly amiss. Upon returning to the spot where he had left his carriage, he found it had disappeared, together with his smart clothes which he had left inside. He rode on horseback to the nearest village and by good luck discovered the missing phaeton outside an inn. Page then showed considerable ingenuity and pluck to recover the carriage without raising suspicion. He took off his outer garments, threw them down a well and rushed, clad in his underwear, into the inn, claiming he had just been robbed, stripped and thrown into a ditch. Inside the inn were some haymakers who had earlier found the carriage and thought it had been abandoned. Page accused them of the theft and the landlord helped to detain them until the authorities could be summoned. The haymakers were later sent for trial but Page refused to give evidence against them, as he had recovered his property, and they were eventually released. The incident persuaded him to dispense with the phaeton on future occasions.

William Page robbing a gentleman on Putney Heath. Note the highwayman's waiting phaeton in background. Engraving c. 1750. (Wandsworth Library, London)

His caution enabled him to survive for another three years as a successful highwayman; a remarkable achievement, considering he participated in some hundred robberies each year. Meanwhile he enjoyed a life of luxury, wearing the most expensive clothes, gambling and staying at fashionable addresses throughout England. His days of freedom, however, were numbered after an accomplice, his boyhood friend John Darwell, held up alone a coach near Sevenoaks, in Kent. Most of the men in the coach were armed and they captured Darwell. In an attempt to save his own neck, he offered to turn king's evidence and betrayed Page, who was apprehended at the 'Golden Lion' in Grosvenor Square, near Hyde Park, in possession of a detailed road map and a black wig. He was placed in Newgate Prison and charged with a highway robbery offence. Lack of evidence gained him an acquittal but he was sent to Maidstone Gaol to face another highway robbery charge. This time he was found guilty and on 6 April 1758 he was hanged, at the age of twenty-eight, at Maidstone.

'SIXTEEN-STRING JACK'

During the final decades of the eighteenth century, the formation of John Fielding's Bow Street Runners made life extremely hazardous for English highwaymen. A good example was John Rann, one of the last extrovert highwaymen to gain fame and notoriety before he was caught by the Runners. He was born in a village near Bath in 1750, the son of an itinerant tinker who placed him in service at the age of twelve. Rann later worked as a footman, before becoming a coachman to several wealthy gentlemen in London. He admired their life-style and began stealing to finance his own high living. He became an extravagant dresser and wore breeches with eight silk strings or tassels attached to each knee. The strings were threaded into the eyelet holes, where the breeches were gathered at the knee. This fashion earned Rann the nickname of 'Sixteen-string Jack'.

His entry into crime was as a pickpocket, working in a team with several other men. The booty he acquired was 'fenced' for him by his mistress, Eleanor Roche. In due course, Rann decided there was more money to be made as a highwayman and took to the road. On one occasion, he was captured after being accused of robbing a coach on the Hounslow Road and stealing a watch and money. He was brought to court in leg-irons, making a flamboyant appearance before John Fielding with blue ribbons tied to his irons and a buttonhole of flowers in his new suit. Eleanor Roche appeared alongside him accused of receiving. Both pleaded their innocence and lack of real evidence secured them their freedom. However, Fielding remained suspicious and detailed one of his best Bow Street Runners to take an interest in their future activities.

Rann continued his highwayman's life and even openly boasted about it to his friends in the many taverns he visited. He dressed extravagantly on social occasions, one of his favourite outfits comprising a scarlet jacket, tambour waistcoat, white silk stockings and a hat trimmed with lace. Once he wore this garb when attending the execution of a fellow highwayman at Tyburn; craving attention, he pushed himself to the front of the crowd in order to be more conspicuous, and it was rumoured that he forecast to all and sundry that one day he would not be just a spectator at Tyburn but the main participant in the proceedings. His outrageous style of dressing made him easily recognisable, too, at the races, when he wore a sporty waistcoat of blue satin, trimmed with silver threads.

Highwayman John Rann, alias 'Sixteen-string Jack', dressed in silk breeches with eight silk tassels around each knee.

When Rann was at work, however, he deliberately dressed shabbily. This confused his many victims and witnesses because they could not vouch it to be the same man who appeared in court extravagantly dressed. He gained several acquittals on this account but the Bow Street Runners were not so easily deceived. They continued to watch Rann carefully, until he made a final mistake.

This occurred on 26 September 1774 when he robbed, with an accomplice, Dr William Bell, a chaplain, as he travelled along the Uxbridge road by Gunnersbury Lane in Middlesex. They stole just eighteen pence from him and a watch in a tortoiseshell case. The latter was to prove fatal, as it was later traced to his mistress Eleanor Roche by the Bow Street Runners. In court, Dr Bell positively identified Rann as the highwayman and this evidence was corroborated by his servant, who saw the accused riding in the area just before the robbery took place. Rann was found guilty and sentenced to be hanged, but mercy was recommended for his accomplice, and Eleanor Roche earned fourteen years' transportation for her part as the 'fence'.

'Sixteen-string Jack' remained cheerful to the end and entertained seven girls among his guests at a party – apparently with much drink and merriment – in the condemned cell, on the Sunday before his execution. Aged twenty-four, he was allowed to go to his execution at Tyburn, on 30 November 1774, dressed in a suit of his best gaudy clothes.

The Bow Street Runners concentrated all their efforts whenever the Royal Mail was robbed. They apprehended the notorious Weston brothers, George and Joseph, after their robbery of the Bristol Mail, tracing them when they retired to London with their booty. Both were hanged at Tyburn in September 1782, the usual penalty for mail robbery.

As the vigilant Runners scored more successes, the highwaymen became ever more desperate. Jerry Abershaw resisted arrest in 1795 and shot one Bow Street Runner dead and seriously injured another. Despite this, he was immediately captured and hanged, aged twenty-two, on Kennington Common. After his execution the authorities hung his body in chains on Putney Heath, where he had frequently robbed before returning to his nearby base at the 'Bald Faced Stag' inn. It was estimated that close on 100,000 people came to view the corpse. He had enjoyed one taste of fame. A popular saying of the day jokingly compared the highwayman to the Prime Minister: 'Abershaw takes their purses with pistols – Pitt with Parliament'.

One of the last notable highwaymen who operated in the London area was James (alias Robert) Snooks. He was a native of Hungerford, in Berkshire, but lodged in Woodstock Street, Marylebone, in London, when committing his thefts. On 17 May

1801, he rode from his lodgings on his grey horse to rob the postboy carrying the mail from Tring to Hemel Hempstead, in Hertfordshire. He got away with over £1500 in cash, a huge sum in those days. The General Post Office offered the exceptionally high reward of £200, in addition to the usual £100 payable by Act of Parliament for apprehending highwaymen. Meanwhile Snooks retired to his home town of Hungerford, but the following year he was betrayed by a former schoolfriend for the reward. He was tried at Hertford Assizes and sentenced to be hanged at the scene of his crime on Boxmoor Common, Hertfordshire. The sentence was carried out in March 1802. Before he died he made a courageous speech, extolling the virtues of observing the Sabbath and always obeying one's parents when young. He stressed that deviation from these two basic principles could lead to all forms of crime in later life. He was buried on Boxmoor Common and a rough-hewn stone, engraved with the name Robert Snooks, marked the spot.

In the same year of 1802, the famous Drury Lane actress, Mrs Dora Jordan, was held up by two black-cloaked highwaymen when travelling in her coach at night near Sittingbourne, Kent. Mrs Jordan was the mistress of the Duke of Clarence, later King William IV, and she bore him several children. At the time of the hold-up, Mrs Jordan was travelling with a clergyman. Fortunately, the highwaymen took fright after a tussle with Mrs Jordan's manservant and galloped off without robbing them.

Although the era of the highwayman had virtually passed in London, it continued for some two or three more decades in the country areas, where there was a sparser force of law officers. Highwaymen here were still being captured, hanged or transported until the end of the 1830s. However, many were frustrated by their victims' growing habit of carrying Bank Port Bills instead of cash. These were the equivalent of Bank of England notes, made payable several days after their issue, thus enabling the sender to stop payment if necessary. Between them, the law enforcers and the banks eventually persuaded highwaymen that their chosen way of life was both unsafe and unprofitable.

— CHAPTER EIGHT —

EUROPEAN BANDITRY

In mainland Europe, in contrast to England, highwaymen seldom operated individually and those who did were rarely of high social status. More common in Europe were the large bands of army deserters, discharged soldiers and smugglers who roamed at will throughout many regions of France, Italy, Spain and Germany. The situation arose because, as a result of wars during the fifteenth to seventeenth centuries, many regions were plagued by extreme poverty. Here, too, many men robbed to survive. Some of the more adventurous types departed in due course to the colonies of the New World in the hope of improving their fortunes and some became buccaneers there.

In fifteenth-century France, gangs of brigands terrorised the countryside, raided towns and attacked travellers. Many of these robber bands were groups of mercenaries discharged from the army after the end of the Hundred Years' War. Because they stripped people of their money, they were called 'Écorcheurs' ('Skinners'). In the following century, much bandit activity took place in the mountainous regions of Central France and the Pyrénées, the roads in these areas being particularly unsafe for travel.

FRENCH BANDITRY

In the early seventeenth century, banditry erupted in the Périgord region of France, where there was much rural unrest. Many of the peasants, after a failed uprising against their landlords, joined a criminal gang under the leadership of Pierre Grellety, who operated from a base hidden in dense woodland. They robbed any rich travellers who ventured along the forest roads, in the manner of England's Robin Hood. Grellety became a local hero and the authorities, having failed to apprehend him, eventually persuaded

him, in 1642, to take up a commission in the army to serve in Italy.

Banditry continued throughout the rest of seventeenth-century France, with many wealthy merchants and tax collectors being robbed and killed, and such lawlessness became extremely widespread by the end of the century. One of several favourite ambush places was where the Paris to Orléans road passed close to the forest of Torfou.

At the beginning of the eighteenth century, one of France's most famous bandits, known as Louis Dominique Bourguignon, known as Cartouche, plagued the environs of Paris. Born in 1693, he was kidnapped as a child by gypsies, who trained him as a thief. At the age of sixteen he joined a band of highway robbers who operated in Paris and on the roads leading into the capital. When the authorities came close to apprehending him, he evaded arrest by joining the army. Later, he deserted after stealing money and rejoined his criminal group in Paris, displaying such talent and courage that in 1717 he became their leader. His nickname of 'Cartouche', meaning 'cartridge' came to be used as a generic term to denote a highwayman.

His many daring exploits brought him notoriety and, because he targeted the rich and powerful (once making a fleeting appearance before them at the Paris Opéra), he gained the admiration of the poorer sections of the public. After surviving several successful years as an outlaw, he was eventually captured. Before his trial, he was incarcerated and chained in a dungeon at the Conciergerie in Paris. After his guilt was proved, he was sentenced to be skinned alive and broken-at-the-wheel on 28 November 1721. It was recorded that just before the execution he was offered a cup of coffee but replied he would much prefer a glass of wine and some bread. He still felt

Popular French bandit Louis Dominique Cartouche in chains at the Conciergerie dungeon in Paris. (Bibliothèque Nationale de France)

certain his men would come to rescue him; when they failed to appear he poured scorn on them and died with great courage.

Perhaps even more famous in French bandit history was the brigand Louis Mandrin, born in St Etienne St Geoirs in the province of Dauphiné in about 1725. At various times he worked as a tax collector and also served in the army. After a while, he deserted both careers to take up a life of crime, which included robbery, murder, extortion and smuggling on a grand scale. His knowledge of

the tax and excise system enabled him to waylay the collectors and to smuggle huge quantities of untaxed tobacco and cheap textiles across the French border – commodities in great demand among the poor.

Louis Mandrin at one time commanded a well-armed bandit gang of about 500 men who fought many bloody battles, against both the excisemen and the army, from whom they stole a large arsenal of weapons which included pistols, muskets with bayonets, and swords. Mandrin and his gang were particularly active along the border of France and Savoy, which was then an independent duchy.

Mandrin's successes largely derived from his popularity with the peasantry, who sheltered him from the authorities. He was regarded as a 'social bandit', a man of poor origins who had proved his ability to survive in a harsh environment. Also to his advantage was the fact that the French 'maréchaussée', or mounted constabulary, then numbered barely 3000 men. This centralised police force could therefore offer only limited assistance and support to the local rural law offi-

cers, who were likewise short of personnel.

Mandrin appeared to possess a near pathological hatred of soldiers and he brutally murdered many of them. Thus in the early 1750s, he set out from the village of Curson with five or six members of his gang and ambushed five soldiers on duty. They shot dead a brigadier and another soldier, and wounded two more, one of whom died later. They stole the soldiers' weapons, the dead officer's horse, his coat and his gold-trimmed hat, which Mandrin subsequently wore. The following day, the group forced their way into a soldier's home, threatened him with death, stole his guns

The well-armed Louis Mandrin – France's most notorious and ruthless bandit and smuggler of the eighteenth century. (Bibliothèque Nationale de France)

and forced his wife to take them to the stable, where they stole his horse. On another occasion, the band attacked a group of guards in their barracks at Pont de le Drac. After gaining admittance through the door, they killed one of the soldiers and injured several others, before stealing their arms and possessions.

The same group of brigands afterwards ambushed troops from the brigade at Taulignan, killing one of them and injuring several others, one of whom died a few days later. Three of the bandits later stayed at an inn in Tioulle, where they shot a sergeant whom they thought was watching them.

In Rovergue they committed several offences, including the killing of a pregnant woman, in whose house a man whom they had been pursuing was attempting to hide. In Rhodez, Mandrin forced a merchant to sell his tobacco at a price he himself fixed, and wrote to the local authorities demanding the surrender of the weapons previously seized from other brigands and kept in the town hall. Shortly afterwards, the gang stole tobacco from a merchant at Mende before travelling to Savoy. On the way they passed St Etienne St Geoirs and sought out a soldier, Sigismond-Jacques Moret, whom Mandrin suspected of having earlier

The main areas of banditry in seventeenth and eighteenth-century France.

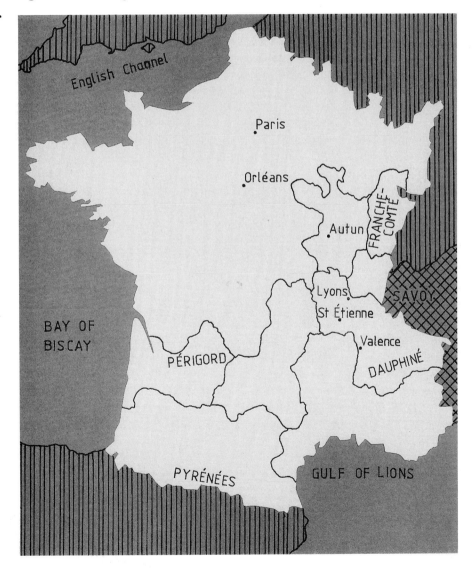

arrested his brother Pierre for forgery, as a result of which he was executed. Mandrin murdered Moret, as well as the eighteen-month-old child he was holding in his arms.

Mandrin then led his band of brigands into the region of Franche-Comté where they robbed, wounded and killed several soldiers. They then coerced two tobacco merchants to hand over money under the pretext of supplying them with stocks of tobacco. At Montbrison, they fought their way into the prison, releasing eleven prisoners, and then ambushed two soldiers from the brigade of Cormaranche and stole the wages they were transporting to pay the guard.

In Savoy, Mandrin and his companions obtained money under false pretences by selling bundles of fake tobacco, and blackmailed several merchants into paying protection money. A fortnight or so later, Mandrin fired at the postilion driving a coach between Lyon and Châlon, injuring one of the horses. The precise reason for the action was not clear but Mandrin was believed to have halted and boarded the coach to search for a particular passenger. Two days later his men fired on a group of soldiers and stole their arms and possessions, including those of their brigadier; they then stormed the premises of a merchant and looted his tobacco, together with his possessions and furniture, wounding two soldiers who were guarding his stock. They next pillaged the homes of several soldiers in various towns, before breaking into eight different prisons to release some of the inmates. Further victims included men of the Harcourt regiment, one of whom was killed, and, the following day, a group of soldiers at Seurre-en-Bourgogne, where they forced open the door of the general's private quarters and stole his possessions.

Mandrin next appeared in Fauxbourg, despatching his men to the town of Beaune, which they entered by breaking open the gates, killing two guards and wounding several others. The bandits then ordered the local mayor to travel to Fauxbourg to meet their chief. Mandrin planned to extort funds from various merchants in Beaune and persuaded the mayor to write to them for the money, which was duly delivered.

He also threatened to scale the walls of the town of Autun with ladders and to ravage and set fire to Fauxbourg to extort additional money. To ensure they were not attacked whilst waiting for the cash, they held several clerics as hostages.

At the village of Grenand, the bandit band fought another battle with soldiers, killing and injuring several officers, dragoons and hussars. They then raided two prisons, releasing over thirty prisoners, who promptly joined them. The brigands then proceeded to steal more horses, arms and equipment from the army and brutally assassinated five soldiers at Breuil, even though several knelt and pleaded for their lives. Shortly afterwards, they murdered a civilian in St Clement because he refused to show them the houses in the town where soldiers lived; on the same day they robbed citizens of money and fired at the door of a brigadier's house, wounding his wife who was standing behind it. She died a few days later.

At long last, the authorities managed to capture Mandrin on Savoy territory, after he had been betrayed. At the subsequent trial, he was found guilty of an immense number of criminal offences and was condemned to be broken-at-the-wheel on 26 May 1755 at Valence, in southeastern France. On the execution day he was led, dressed in a shirt with a rope around his neck, to the front of the cathedral. He was made to carry a banner with words in large letters proclaiming him as 'Chef des Contrebandiers, Criminels de Lèze-Majesté, Assassins, Voleurs et Perturbateurs du Repos Public' ('Leader of Smugglers, Treasonous Persons, Assassins, Thieves and Disturbers of the Peace.') He knelt bare-headed before the cathedral, holding a large burning candle and was given the opportunity to beg forgiveness from God for his many crimes. He was then driven in a cart to the scaffold where the executioner broke his arms, legs, thighs and back with a metal bar. He was placed on a wheel, with his face turned skywards until he was dead.

Afterwards, the French writer Voltaire, who conducted a lifelong campaign against injustice and intolerance, surprisingly highlighted Louis

French bandit Louis Mandrin shackled in prison at Valence, awaiting execution; insert shows him later being beaten to death. (Bibliothèque Nationale de France)

Mandrin's reputation as a social bandit, ignoring the extremely brutal and violent nature of his lengthy catalogue of criminal activities. Voltaire's judgement was probably clouded by his opposition to the royal autocracy and aristocratic privileges of the day. Possibly he classified the judges, who had condemned Mandrin, as part of that same feudal social structure.

Later in the eighteenth century, despite the increased strength of the 'maréchaussée', it still proved difficult to control the large numbers of bandits and especially those known as 'faux saulniers', who specialised in breaking the state's salt monopoly. At the end of the century, many young men were forced into a life of banditry after fleeing from the army recruiting officers. At the conclusion of the French Revolution there were numerous outlaw gangs, some of whom terrorised and tortured their victims by holding their feet over fires, until they revealed the whereabouts of their wealth. These gangs gained the nickname of 'chauffeurs' ('warmers' or 'stokers') and they thrived in France because the authorities were more concerned with the aftermath of the internal conflict and recent horrors

of the Reign of Terror under Robespierre than to worry about individual bands of outlaws. Despite this, a few robbers were caught and those that escaped execution were often branded 'TF' ('travaux forcés') and sent to work as galley slaves, chained together to row the heavy oars of French ships. This punishment continued until 1832 and was not reserved exclusively for outlaws. Servants who committed crimes in their masters' households were likewise branded and sent to the galleys.

On 27 April 1796, when France was still recovering from the revolution, there was a particularly brutal night-time robbery of the Lyon Mail, after it left Paris. On the following morning, the mail-coach was found abandoned at the roadside, near the village of Lieursaint. The driver lay dead in his seat with wounds to his chest and his throat cut so badly that the head was nearly severed from the trunk. The postilion lay dead on the road with savage head and chest wounds. Letters were found scattered in the vicinity of the coach and the highwaymen who perpetrated the atrocity escaped with 75,000 livres (about £3000) in bank bills and silver.

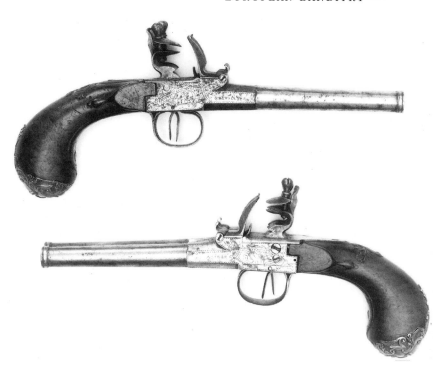

For terrified European travellers in fear of highwaymen, this late eighteenth-century pair of double-barrelled flintlock pistols offered the opportunity of four individual shots before reloading. The weapons shown were made in Belgium at the great arms production centre of Liège. (Courtesy of Sotheby's)

The tragedy of the two brutally murdered mail-coach men was compounded by the fact that an innocent man named Joseph Lesurques was later to be executed for the crime. His unlucky involvement in the incident took place purely by chance, after he had inherited some money and moved from the country, with his wife and children, to live in Paris. After the unloading of his family's household effects from a hired conveyance, Lesurques apparently walked to the Paris office of the carrier to pay the removal bill. He was on friendly terms with the head of the carrier firm because both originally came from the same village. The next day they arranged to have a meal together and while at the restaurant, they casually conversed with two strangers.

A few days later Joseph Lesurques unexpectedly encountered the carrier again while strolling in Paris. The latter was on his way to the magistrate's office on business and, as he had time to spare, Lesurques volunteered to accompany him. When they arrived, some people were present in the magistrate's office who were being questioned about the earlier Lyon mail robbery; so Lesurques and his friend waited in the adjoining office. The

visitors were members of the serving staff at an inn, near the scene of the hold-up, and had been brought as witnesses by the police to Paris, after reporting that a gang of horsemen had called at the inn just before the mail-coach arrived to change horses. They believed that their earlier customers might well have been the guilty highwaymen. While in the magistrate's office, a couple of them glanced by chance into the office next door. They then astounded the magistrate by stating excitedly that two of the highwaymen were sitting outside his office. The men they accused were Lesurques, whom they swore they could not fail to recognise, and the carrier. As a consequence, Joseph Lesurques and his friend were held on suspicion of highway robbery and murder.

Two other suspects had earlier been arrested, after their hired horses, later found to have been used in the robbery, were returned to their stable in Paris, in a highly distressed condition. The stable owner reported the incident to the police, and the witnesses from the inn identified these two as members of the group who had called at their hostelry before the robbery. They proved to be the very strangers with whom Lesurques and his friend had innocently spoken in the Paris restaurant. Eventually, after further investigation, all four men were sent for trial, only the carrier being acquitted, as he had a firm alibi that was easily verified in court. The other three were found guilty of the mail robbery and the murders. They were condemned to be executed, despite the other two swearing that Lesurques was never involved in the crime. The death sentence by guillotine was carried out on all three men on 10 March 1797. Lesurques dressed himself completely in white, as a final despairing token of his innocence. The two others pleaded again on the scaffold that he had not been a member of their gang but admitted he bore a remarkable likeness to one of their missing accomplices, named Dubosq. Their pleas were of no avail and Lesurques died at the age of thirty-three years. His wife and children were left in much distress, as his property, according to procedure, was seized. A few years later, the police arrested Dubosq on another charge and eventually proved

A busy European coaching scene – coaches were robbed by individual highwaymen on the Continent but to a lesser extent than in England. Painting by Charles Cooper Henderson. c. 1830. (British Sporting Art Trust)

he had also taken part in the Lyon mail robbery. The authorities acknowledged they had tragically executed, due to double coincidence, an innocent man. Unfortunately, the authorities did nothing to help his wife and children, despite the miscarriage of justice.

ITALIAN BANDITRY

In Italy the long history of banditry surpassed that of France and all other European countries. The Italian 'banditos' operated mainly in mountainous and rural regions, due to the many available hiding places and the greater chance of defending themselves successfully against the army or the police. Typical sites were Calabria in the southern

'toe' of Italy and Apulia, with its hilly central area, in the 'heel'. The mountainous island of Sicily also had a long history of banditry and kidnapping for ransom, as had the island of Corsica, with its rugged coastline and mountainous interior. Although Corsica has owed political allegiance to France since 1768, it has always retained much in common with Italy. The Corsican people have a long history of comparative poverty, local family feuds and misgivings about accepting laws imposed on them. As a consequence, islanders often regarded bandit leaders as heroes.

Banditry in Sicily, too, has always been difficult to suppress, especially in the eighteenth century when taxation was extremely high and land

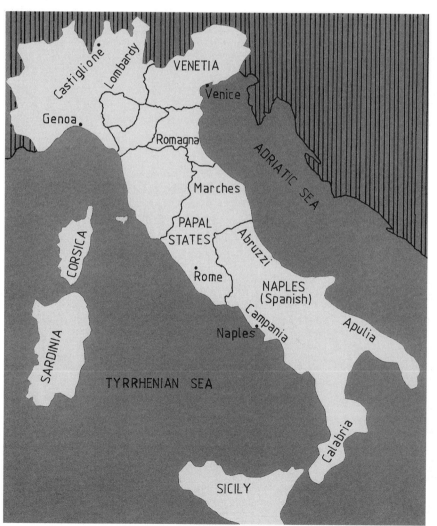

Left: Banditry occurred over areas of sixteenth- to eighteenth-century Italy, when it was divided into a number of separate states.

Right: Italian bandit Benedetto Mangone (a forerunner of Marco Sciarra) holding-up the famous poet Torquato Tasso and his party and then allowing them to proceed unhindered.

tenure impossible for the poor. A ban on the carrying of weapons introduced at that time failed completely to reduce the level of crime. The situation was also aggravated by a secret society, first formed in the thirteenth century, which developed into a symbol of protest against Neapolitan misrule and later into a much feared criminal organisation. In the nineteenth century, this became known as the mafia ('bragging' or 'swanking', in Italian dialect) after the great landowners in Sicily employed it to manage their affairs. The organisation held vast power in Sicily and the authorities were much hampered in fighting it by its code of absolute silence.

Despite the wealthy few, the vast majority of Sicilians remained poor. On mainland Italy, factors other than rural poverty assisted the general growth of banditry. Until the mid-nineteenth century, the centre of the country was divided into a series of separate small Papal States, which made it easy for the bandits to flee across borders to safety when pursued. Moreover, French military incursions into Italy caused many men to join the bandit gangs, as a token of patriotism and resistance against the invaders, whom they sometimes robbed and killed.

In the latter part of the sixteenth century, bandits infested the Campania region around Naples. Measures attempted by the authorities to control them included the burning of large areas of bushes and trees to remove natural cover and drive them into the open, as well as the building of high observation towers around Naples, to gain early warning of their approach. The outlaws were often supported and sheltered by the feudal nobles, some of whom actually operated as great bandit lords themselves, in defiance of the Papal States. As a consequence, the Pope instigated severe counter-measures, which resulted in many being captured and executed. Among these was the Duke of Montemarciano, Alfonso Piccolomini, who for thirteen years controlled a large army of bandits in the Romagna region, until he was captured in 1591 and executed in Florence. The Grand Duke Ramberto Malatesta earlier suffered a similar fate in 1587 for his bandit activities.

One of the most famous bandits of this period was Marco Sciarra, who was a native of Castiglione, in Lombardy. At one time he headed a bandit band of about 600 men who rampaged over a wide area, including the Romagna and the Marches regions of eastern Italy, from his base at Abruzzi. His men also controlled large sections of countryside around Rome and even held their own courts and marriage ceremonies. Sciarra was much admired by the poor because he sometimes distributed his stolen wealth among them. The people of Naples treated him as a hero, hoping that one day he would gain control of their city to free them from the ruling Spanish viceroy.

After almost seven years as a successful bandit leader, Marco Sciarra made the mistake of

The capture of Italian bandit Don Ciro Anicchiarico. The siege took place at a fortified farmhouse at Scaserba, about 10 miles from Francavilla. Don Ciro resisted the soldiers' attack until he was exhausted and finally surrendered. His execution took place by firing squad in 1818, by being shot in the back, the normal procedure for thieves.

departing to the Republic of Venice, after being harassed by the authorities. Papal pressure on Venice then resulted in his betrayal, by leading him into a trap when he left Venice to visit friends near Naples; he was murdered there by one of his confederates in 1593.

Sciarra may have modelled his lifestyle on another earlier sixteenth-century Italian bandit, Benedetto Mangone, who once showed a sensitive side to his nature when his bandit gang waylaid a party of travellers, which included the well-known Italian poet, Torquato Tasso. Apparently, as a mark of respect for the poet and his work, he allowed the party to proceed unharmed. Mangone was eventually apprehended and executed by being beaten to death in Naples.

The law began briefly to get the upper hand when some bandit bands started to rob the peasantry, losing their support and protection. Many of the leaders were betrayed, captured or assassinated.

After a period of comparative calm, the invasion of Italy by Napoleon Bonaparte in 1796–7 brought an upsurge in banditry thanks to new recruits joining for patriotic reasons. One bandit leader, Fra Diavolo, became a national hero due to his fierce resistance against the French, until he was captured by them and executed. After the fall of Napoleon and the return of Ferdinand I as King of Naples, bandit activity again declined for a time, mainly because of the success of the army and police in gaining public support. The police also started to gather intelligence on the movements of suspected criminals, by keeping a close watch on reported strangers in certain areas. As a result, the notorious bandit priest, Don Ciro Anicchiarico, was captured, admitting at his trial that he had murdered at least seventy people. The respite, however, was temporary, and bandit activity increased once more until the Italian Government regained control towards the end of the nineteenth century, after the dissolution of the separate Papal States and the unification of the country. Nevertheless, banditry was still difficult to eradicate because poor people made money by selling food and supplies to the bandits, some of whom also received the protection of powerful corrupt officials.

SPANISH BANDITRY

Spain, like Italy, was invaded by Napoleon, and here, too, recruits flocked to the ranks of bandit groups, determined to resist the French. Unfortunately, many who joined out of patriotism remained after the withdrawal of the enemy to continue their lives as members of the 'bandoleros'. The two main areas of bandit activity in Spain were Catalonia, the mainly mountainous region of north-east Spain, on the Mediterranean, and the region below the Sierra Morena mountain range, in southern Spain. Again the topography of these areas afforded bandits relatively safe hiding places. In some parts of the countryside, the bandits held greater powers than the government. Many of the rural nobility were also involved in banditry, as they were in Italy.

Catalan banditry reached a peak at the end of the sixteenth century – a time of brutal peasant suppression. Bandit leaders became heroes when they raided the estates of wealthy landowners. The fame of one of them, Perot Rocaguinarda, was further enhanced by the Spanish novelist Miguel de Cervantes, who later featured him as Roque Guinart in the second part of his novel *Don Quixote* (1615). Rocaguinarda was especially respected because he never damaged or robbed the church and was always courteous to his victims. He survived as a bandit leader from 1602 until 1611, when he accepted a pardon, on condition he served abroad with the army in Italy. Other Spanish bandits displayed complex personalities by mingling crime and murder with religion and occasional charity to the poor. One of them, for example, always placed a crucifix on the graves of his victims.

A wide-scale outbreak of banditry flared up in Catalonia as a result of the War of the Spanish Succession (1701–14). It was eventually brought under control, thanks mainly to the efforts of a country gentleman named Pedro Veciana, who organised an armed force from among his farm workers and servants to resist bandit attacks, and

The main areas of banditry in sixteenth to nineteenth-century Spain.

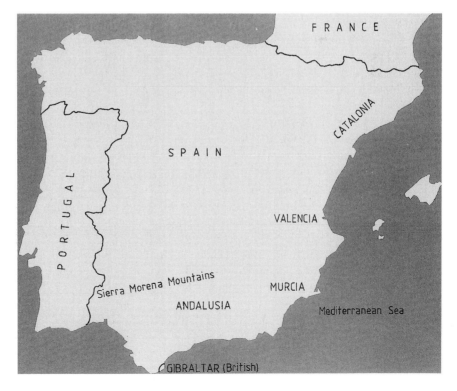

persuaded fellow landowners to do likewise. Their combined private army became known as the 'Mozos' ('Boys') of Veciana, and such was the success of these armed vigilantes that the government asked Veciana to form a special permanent police corps, known as the 'Escuadra de Cataluna'.

In the following century, around 1844, the Duke of Ahumada raised a further complementary constabulary force, known as 'La Guardia Civil', which further reduced the number of brigands. The local Catalonian population not only supported the new law enforcement bodies but also sometimes took the law into their own hands. In 1874, for example, an angry group of workers attacked a group of bandits at the ruined castle site of San Martin de Centellas and beat them to death with their cudgels.

The bandits who operated below the Sierra Morena mountain range in southern Spain also remained active for many centuries. The local people tolerated them and especially so after the War of the Spanish Succession, when Gibraltar was formally ceded to Britain, by the Treaty of Utrecht in 1713. Some bandits later smuggled tobacco, supported by a few of the more lawless local residents. One such smuggler and bandit in the nineteenth century was José Maria, made famous by the French composer Georges Bizet, who with a sense of dramatic realism used a character based on him, from a story by Prosper Mérimée, in his opera *Carmen*. In real life, José Maria took part in the liberal uprising against the repressive policies of the King of Spain, Ferdinand VII, before he became a smuggler and bandit. He was later bribed by the government to give up his criminal career and gather a force to suppress other groups of bandits, one of whom eventually shot and killed him as he attempted an arrest. As the century progressed, the government were forced to send large contingents of the army to southern Spain to control these outlaws.

Although the vast majority of bandits were ruthless criminals who terrorised the districts they roamed, it was the few who behaved in a more gentlemanly fashion who were best remembered. In the early seventeenth century, one group of Spanish bandits in Andalusia, the south-ernmost region of the country, always dressed in elegant clothes, spoke courteously and never stole more than half of their victims' wealth, for which behaviour they became known as the 'Holy Ones'. Later in the century, other bandit groups operating to the east of Andalusia likewise refrained from stripping clean or murdering their victims, also invariably paying their debts of honour when they owed villagers money for food supplied to them in hard times.

OTHER EUROPEAN COUNTRIES

Elsewhere in Europe – Germany, the Balkans, Greece and Russia – bandits through the centuries have at various times embarrassed governments, whose draconian measures against the outlaws they caught failed to deter those who survived. In Germany, during the sixteenth and seventeenth centuries, highway robbers were left to rot on roadside gallows; others were abandoned while still alive, to die in agony, strapped to the wheels on which their bones had already been smashed with iron bars. In Germany, hanging was considered a shameful way to die and the method was usually reserved for robbers and other criminals of low birth. People of higher social status were usually beheaded. This was done without a block and axe; the prisoner simply knelt and the executioner swung his huge sword, death occurring after one blow if his aim and strength were good. Men who had persistently robbed were usually killed by the agonising method of breaking-at-the-wheel. One of the longest-serving executioners in Germany was Franz Schmidt, who officiated at Nuremberg from 1578 to 1617.

During the period from about 1570 to 1650, even the poor in Germany were fearful of venturing on to the roads outside their villages and towns. The princes who ruled the land eventually met together and decided to employ an army of spies, including some innkeepers, to report on the movements of strangers in their areas. In the mid-seventeenth century, the former Prussian province of Brandenburg became infested with bandits, and the efficient local militia eventually gained the upper hand only by a combination of ruthless executions and forcible recruitment of offenders. In contrast, the absence of an efficient military or police force enabled Johann Buckler, alias Schindler-Hannes or 'Jack the Skinner', to thrive as an outlaw in Germany between 1797 and 1802. Buckler was born in Muklen on the Rhine and specialised in robbing Jews. He was eventually captured and executed by being beheaded.

In Russia, inadequate policing also encouraged much banditry. During the eighteenth century, no national police force existed and troops were often used to maintain order. They summarily executed any bandits caught and even fairly minor offenders were punished by whipping at the scenes of their crimes. There was an ethnic basis to certain outbreaks of outlawry, as exemplified by the Cossack groups who plundered in response to the expansion of Russia in the seventeenth and eighteenth centuries. Many peasants fled the harsh feudal system and joined the brigands to rob rich travellers.

Similarly, when the Balkan peninsula was under Turkish Ottoman rule, many peasants joined the bandit groups as a token of Christian revolt against the Turks. Official authorisation for some members of the public to carry weapons in order to deter the bandits had the reverse effect to that intended; the armed citizens, called 'armatoli', aided and protected the outlaws and sometimes even joined them.

Greece has also had a long history of endemic banditry which often took the form of kidnapping for ransom. After the country first gained its independence in 1829 from Turkish Ottoman rule, several of the newly appointed officials unscrupulously used some of the bandit groups to increase their power bases. The army was later brought in to exercise stricter control but banditry was never completely eradicated. In 1870, for example, a party of rich English travellers were ambushed and captured at Oropus, near Marathon, a few miles north-east of Athens. Two members of the group, Lord and Lady Muncaster, were later freed so that they could arrange the payment of a £25,000 ransom. In the meantime, the government decided to hunt the bandits down and rescue the hostages but the plan misfired; the bandits murdered the remaining hostages before they themselves were apprehended and executed. Also, in 1928, Greek bandits captured two former government officials in the Epirus region of western Greece and obtained a large ransom for their release.

Finally, it is worth recording the exploits of an Irishman, James Butler, born in Kilkenny in

Decapitation, an execution method used in Germany for many centuries. The highwayman Johann Buckler was beheaded in this way in 1802.

1690, who committed robberies in many European countries, including Spain, Italy, France and Holland and ended his days in England. His hard-working and honest father despaired when he found his son stealing at an early age. Later, seeking adventure, Butler joined the army in Galway, was sent to Spain and promptly deserted to the opposing Spanish army, learning to speak fluent Spanish and apparently other European languages. Later, he robbed a Spanish army captain of a considerable sum of money before fleeing to Andalusia, a part of the country well away from the scene of the theft. Butler soon spent his ill-gotten gains and to obtain further funds posed as a foreign physician, dispensing and selling 'wonder-cure' medicines, and robbing one lady of some gold and her jewels when she came for a consultation before he left for Italy.

He quickly spent the money after arriving in Venice. In order to rectify the situation, he volunteered to disclose the secret of the philosopher's stone but the venture proved unsuccessful. Undeterred, Butler joined a group of bandits who one day waylaid a friar; to their astonishment, he was carrying a large fortune in gold and jewels. It was later revealed that he had stolen this booty from King James II's consort and had therefore become a fugitive himself. After the robbery, the friar was never seen again and the bandits could well have murdered him. Because he was a new recruit, Butler's share of the proceeds was small; so he left his companions to try his luck in Florence.

Upon arrival, he went to see an execution of a robber and by chance got into conversation with a gentleman spectator, who evidently summed up the Irishman's roguish character and invited him for a drink in a nearby tavern. He asked Butler whether he would be interested in earning 500 pieces of gold for murdering his rich elderly uncle, so that he could inherit his estate. Butler agreed and took a small money advance before setting out to find an accomplice. He knew where a former member of the 'banditti' lived in Florence and invited him to assist in the venture.

The pair later broke into the old uncle's house at night and brutally murdered him in bed. They placed the corpse in a sack and carried it to the nephew to claim the rest of the promised money. Digging a deep hole to bury the body, it occurred to them that the nephew might betray them in the future, so they attacked and killed him, placing his body in the same grave as his uncle. Then, to ensure his confederate would not be tempted to do likewise, Butler also murdered him, throwing the body into the same hole and covered all three with soil. With the blood of three murders on his hands, he decided it was time to leave Italy for France. In Paris, he joined a gang of thieves who operated in the suburb of St Marcel and participated in several thefts. After robbing a wealthy student of his money and belongings, Butler decided to leave his colleagues and rode off to Holland.

Several miles outside Rotterdam, he caught up with a lady who was travelling alone on her horse, a most unusual occurrence. She was also bound for Rotterdam and evidently they became quite friendly on the way. As darkness approached they stayed at an inn for the night, the landlord assuming they were man and wife. Butler apparently drank heavily during the evening and slept soundly. Waking very late the following morning, he asked the landlord the whereabouts of the lady and was informed she had ridden away several hours previously. Realising she would not return, he then found to his dismay that she had stolen his gold from a case in his room and had also taken his horse, leaving her inferior animal behind. Greatly incensed, Butler sold the horse and with the proceeds paid his fare to England.

In order to obtain immediate funds, Butler turned highwayman and for his first venture held up a coach in Gray's Inn Road, London. Later, after a few narrow escapes, he joined forces with another highwayman. However, the alliance proved short-lived and shortly afterwards, in 1716, both were apprehended in Holloway, convicted and sentenced to be executed at Tyburn. When the hangman carried out his duty, Butler was twenty-eight years old. He was buried in St Andrew's churchyard, Holborn after a dastardly criminal career which had taken him through many of the countries of Europe.

— CHAPTER NINE —

AMERICAN WESTERN OUTLAWS

Few highway robbers existed in America before the nineteenth century. More common were the river pirates who plagued the Ohio and Mississippi, busy routes for both commercial and passenger traffic. The pirates boarded the river flatboats, often murdered their crews and then scuttled the boats after robbing the passengers and seizing the cargoes. A cave known as the Cave-in-Rock on the Ohio River in Hardin County, Illinois, became the operating base for such brigands as Philip Aston, who dressed in lace and ruffles when robbing boats, Samuel Mason, and the bloodthirsty Harpe brothers. Farther south down the river, James Ford successfully combined the conflicting roles of justice of the peace, ferry operator and river pirate chief. He ran ferries on the Ohio River, his men robbed them and he protected the miscreants in court when they were arrested.

Mason and his gang attacked boats both on the Ohio and Mississippi. He also became one of the earliest highwaymen along the Natchez Trace, an old Indian trail where later a 500-mile road running from Nashville, Tennessee to Natchez on the Mississippi River was constructed. After floating their produce southward down the river, settlers and traders travelled by foot or horseback along the trail, mainly in a northerly direction through dense thicket and swamp. They journeyed back by land because their boats could only be poled tediously northward upstream. If they escaped attack by the river pirates on the downward river journey, they ran a high risk of being robbed on the return overland trip. Although Samuel Mason was killed by two of his own men in 1804, others swiftly took his place and the Natchez Trace remained a dangerous place for several decades.

The Harpe brothers, Micajah ('Big Harpe') and Wiley ('Little Harpe'), also robbed along the Natchez Trace and in Kentucky and Tennessee. The brothers were probably insane, as they murdered on the slightest pretext. On one occasion, 'Big Harpe' killed Major John Love merely because he snored too loudly. The brothers also murdered women and children and often dismembered their victims' bodies. Eventually, 'Big Harpe' was killed by vigilantes in 1799 and one of them, in revenge for his wife who had been murdered by the brothers, severed his head and nailed it to a tree on the Natchez Trace. After his brother's death, the younger brother joined the Samuel Mason gang of highwaymen. In 1804, 'Little Harpe' was captured, convicted and legally hanged.

Another notorious bandit, John A. Murrell, born in Tennessee the same year that 'Little Harpe' died, also terrorised travellers along the Natchez Trace and later claimed to have controlled a huge robber gang, which operated over eight states of the southern Middle West. John Murrell also traded criminally in slaves, stealing or encouraging the negroes to abscond from their plantation owners and then selling them to other plantations many miles away. He often stole them anew and resold them time and again. When individual slaves became too well known by being widely advertised as absconders, Murrell would sometimes murder them. In the 1830s, he plotted to incite a widespread slave rebellion. Many northerners, who supported the abolition of slavery, gave their tacit support, not realising that Murrell's real intention was to establish a robber empire by recruiting the freed slaves for his band of highwaymen. When the plot was revealed, in 1834, bringing retribution, some twenty of Murrell's men were hunted down, captured and executed. He himself was apprehended and sentenced to ten years' imprisonment, which he served in Nashville penitentiary. After his release, he died of consumption (pulmonary tuberculosis), in 1844.

The Mississippi River and the settlements that grew along its banks continued to attract outlaws and gamblers throughout most of the nineteenth century. In 1811, the first steamboat, the *New Orleans*, built in Pittsburgh, appeared on the river and brought increased prosperity to the region. The towns along the banks then relied on the regular arrival of freight and passengers. Owners of the picturesque steamboats decorated their vessels with ornate fittings and hostesses at the bars entertained travellers. The steamboat captains allowed professional gamblers to play on their vessels, on condition they received a share of the profits. On-board gambling became a popular pastime and many naive passengers were duped. The carrying of large bank rolls also attracted the attention of outlaws, who followed potential victims after they disembarked. Even on board the combination of liquor, gambling and the carrying of six-guns guaranteed that violence could erupt at any time.

GOLD ROBBERS

In the 1840s, the discovery of gold in California catalysed a large-scale outbreak of outlawry. Prominent among the early bandits was Joaquin Murrieta, probably born in Mexico in about 1832, who arrived in California with his wife around 1849. Facts about him are elusive, although he later attained hero status among the Mexicans living in California. He joined the gold rush but shortly afterwards, in 1850, the white American miners pressed for legislation, known as the 'Grease Act' and the 'Foreign Miners Act' to expel Mexicans from the goldfields. As a consequence, Murrieta started to rob gold mines and hold up stage-coaches, claiming that his band of outlaws only stole and murdered to avenge the way the Spanish-speaking Mexicans in California were abused by the immigrant white American settlers. He terrorised the state for about three

years, until 1853 when a $4000 reward was offered for his capture, dead or alive. Murrieta and his bandits were shortly afterwards ambushed by law enforcement officers led by Texas Ranger Captain Harry Love at Panoche Pass, to the west of Tolare Lake. They did not attempt to take Murrieta alive but killed him with three of his accomplices; two others were captured, although several managed to escape. As proof that they had killed the outlaw leader, the law officers cut off his head and preserved it in alcohol to show to the authorities and other officials. Although it was difficult to verify the identification, the bandit raids ceased, suggesting that the Texas Rangers had got their man.

Many other outlaws operated for several decades in California and stage-coach robberies became a particular problem because they often carried gold ore and dust. The best-known type of coach was the Concord, constructed by the Abbot-Downing Company of Concord, New Hampshire. These vehicles were intended to carry eight or nine passengers inside and two on top, with pro-

A typical stage of the Concord type used by express companies on the overland trails. Soldiers on top guard against possible attack by Indians or outlaws. (National Archives, Maryland, USA)

vision for freight and mail. For stability, they were designed with a low centre of gravity, equidistant between the wheels. The bodywork was made watertight, so that they could be floated across swollen rivers if necessary. When travelling across rough terrain, teams of six mules were used to pull them instead of horses. The coaches were usually accompanied by heavily armed guards. Despite this, an outlaw gang led by 'Reelfoot' Williams gained the first sizeable haul, worth about $7500, by ambushing a stage-coach in 1852.

This sum was dwarfed by 'Rattlesnake' Dick Barter who followed his taking of $80,000 in gold dust from a single stage-coach in 1855 by robbing another of $26,000 the following year. In addition, outlaws held up individual mounted riders who worked for the express companies, in the hope they were carrying gold. Barter even way-laid groups of mounted men who travelled together along the trails, believing there was safety in numbers. Another highwayman, Tom Bell, also became notorious for his robberies of stage-coaches, until he was finally captured and hanged in 1856. Californian highwayman Charles E. Boles, alias 'Black Bart', was held in some respect and noted for his courteous and non-violent nature. He successfully held up some thirty stage-coaches with his shotgun, without firing it once. He was eventually arrested by law enforcement officers in the late 1870s.

The discovery of gold in Idaho in 1860 and Montana in 1863 brought about a situation similar to that experienced earlier in California. Thanks to the lure of easy riches, lawlessness grew at an alarming rate. Miners and stage-coaches transporting gold ore from the Clearwater diggings in Idaho were subjected to frequent attacks. Several

The lynching of John Heith at Tombstone, Arizona on Feb. 22, 1884. He was implicated in a store robbery in which one woman and three men were killed. (National Archives, Maryland, USA)

gang of ruthless outlaws terrorised the trails around the gold-digging towns and robbed stage-coaches, mining company vehicles and individual miners carrying gold dust. Within a year of the discovery of gold in Montana more than one hundred violent deaths occurred. Crime reached such proportions that leading business men and citizens formed vigilante groups. As a result, they summarily executed by hanging twenty-four outlaws between December 1863 and December 1864, among them Plummer. This draconian retribution action virtually eliminated outlawry in Montana.

Lynching of outlaws continued for several more decades in many other areas of the American West and reached a peak in 1884. For example, John Heith was hanged at Tombstone, Arizona on 22 February 1884 for taking part in a robbery two months earlier at the Goldwater-Castaneda store. Other members of his gang were caught and legally hanged on 6 March 1884. Miscarriages of justice also took place at Tombstone, as indicated by one graveyard sign at the nearby cemetery on Boot Hill stating:

'HERE LIES GEORGE JOHNSON, HANGED BY MISTAKE 1882. HE WAS RIGHT, WE WAS WRONG. WE STRUNG HIM UP AND NOW HE'S GONE.'

Another graveyard sign denotes further violent death:

'HERE LIES LESTER MORE. FOUR SLUGS FROM A .44. NO LESS, NO MORE.'

of the desperadoes from Idaho later moved on to Montana, when gold was discovered at Bannack and Grasshopper Creek, a tributary of the Beaverhead River, and at Alder Gulch.

One of the most notorious outlaws in these areas was Henry Plummer, who had previously committed bank robbery. He managed to become the elected sheriff of the tough mining settlements at Bannack and Alder Gulch, supposedly to impose some form of law and order. In reality, his

The discovery of gold in the Black Hills of South Dakota in 1876 again attracted the attention of outlaws, despite most of the gold-carrying stage-coaches being extremely well guarded by expert shotgun riders, with considerable fire-power. The outlaw gang of Wall and Blackburn carried out many stage-coach robberies, as did Sam Bass, with less success. The latter had arrived in South Dakota with four others, after driving a herd of cattle to the Black Hills. Bass who was to become extremely well known and notorious as a train robber in Texas during the following years, was born on 21 July 1851 near Mitchell, Lawrence County, Indiana the son of farming parents who had nine other children. His mother died when he was ten years old; his father married again but died about four years later. An uncle then took guardianship of the children and sent them to school, which Bass hated. At the age of eighteen, he left home, worked in a mill for a short time before departing to Texas where he worked honestly, first in a hotel and then as a cowboy and teamster in Denton. He started to frequent saloons and gamble and became friendly with a small-time crook named Joel Collins. This acquaintance led Bass in 1875 to become a horse thief before he graduated to stage-coach robbery the following year, in the Black Hills.

Bass and four others next tried their hand on the railroad, holding up a Union Pacific train at Big Springs, Nebraska in 1877. This met with mixed success; although they took $60,000 in gold coins from the express car and a further $5000 from the passengers, they were pursued and all were killed except Bass himself. He returned to Denton where he gathered together another band to carry out further train robberies. Most of these were unsuccessful and several of the gang were killed in various encounters with the Texas Rangers. Many of the survivors then deserted Bass, until eventually he was left with only two men. They were joined by another named Jim Murphy, a former acquaintance, who infiltrated the gang with the intention of betraying Bass to the Texas Rangers, with whom he worked in collusion. A trap was set when Bass attempted to rob the bank at Round Rock and a company of Texas Rangers moved in and shot him. Bass died

An express car robbery on the Union Pacific Railway. Woodcut by Western Engr. Co. in 'Hands Up' by Alfred Rasmus Sorenson, 1887. (Library of Congress, LC-USZ62-39654)

on his birthday at the age of twenty-seven, in 1878. The inscription on his tombstone read:

'A BRAVE MAN REPOSES IN DEATH HERE.
WHY WAS HE NOT TRUE?'

The discovery of silver in Nevada in the mid-1870s and the various mining camps which evolved as a consequence, resulted in a spate of robberies carried out by other desperadoes. These were mainly confined to stage-coaches, but trains were also sometimes robbed in Nevada. For instance, 'Big' Jack Davis and his gang boarded a train when it stopped for water, broke into the safe and disappeared with about $35,000, no violence being used in the theft. Afterwards, Davis and his men became lavish spenders in the saloons and this eventually led to their downfall. They were arrested, convicted and sent to a penitentiary for long terms of imprisonment, although Davis was pardoned after serving only about five years. Upon release, he resumed his criminal ways and he was killed in 1874, while attempting to rob a stage-coach.

Another notorious Nevada outlaw, Milton C. Sharp, took no chances with the booty he stole, as he trusted nobody. He always worked alone when holding up stage-coaches and immediately buried the loot. His hidden caches were never discovered after his arrest and imprisonment, although it was rumoured that the early pardon he gained might have been influenced by money from one of the caches.

The four Reno brothers, who drifted into crime during the American Civil War (1861–5), were among the earliest gangs to attempt railroad robbery when, in October 1866, they boarded a train in Indiana, forcing the guard at gun-point to give them the keys of the safe which they proceeded to rob of $13,000. During the following two years, the Reno brothers robbed several other trains and banks until eventually they were tracked down and arrested by Pinkerton detectives. While awaiting trial, vigilantes seized the brothers and lynched them, except for John, who by chance escaped their wrath.

THE JESSE JAMES GANG

It was the aftermath of the Civil War, too, that saw the arrival on the criminal scene of one of the most famous of American outlaws, Jesse Woodson James, who was born on 5 September 1847 in Clay County, Missouri, four years after his elder brother, Alexander Franklin (Frank). Their father was a Baptist minister, the Reverend Robert James, who died when they were young, whereupon their mother, Zerelda, married Dr Reuben Samuel in 1855. In the early days of the war, the James family suffered badly at the hands of the Union forces because of their support for the southern cause. As a result, Frank James joined the guerrilla forces of C. W. Quantrill, fighting as a Confederate irregular against the Union forces. During his service he became friends with Thomas Coleman (Cole) Younger, who later also became an outlaw. Jesse James, just turned fifteen, soon followed his brother's example and joined a similar guerrilla band, under 'Bloody' Bill Anderson. In action, Jesse became noted for his daring and marksmanship. However, he was brutalised by the conflict and once participated in the massacre of twenty-four unarmed Union soldiers.

When the war ended, Jesse rode into Lexington, Missouri to surrender under the protection of a flag of truce. Shortly afterwards, he was treacherously shot and severely wounded in the lung by Federal soldiers. He recovered but found it impossible to get a job in Missouri, as he had fought against the Unionists. As a result, so he later claimed, he had no alternative but to become an outlaw and he was joined in the venture by his brother Frank. At the time, the brothers lived with their mother and helped on her farm.

By this time banks, too, were popular targets for robbers. Jesse committed his first daylight robbery of a bank on 13 February 1866 when he, his brother Frank and eight other men rode into Liberty, Missouri to carry out the hold-up. The following year, Jesse became leader of the 'James' gang who, for the next ten years or so, continued to rob banks, stage-coaches and trains, from Iowa to Alabama and Texas. Belle Starr, 'The Bandit Queen', also joined the gang for a time. Their first

Frank James, the elder brother of Jesse James. (Library of Congress, LC-USZ62-38208)

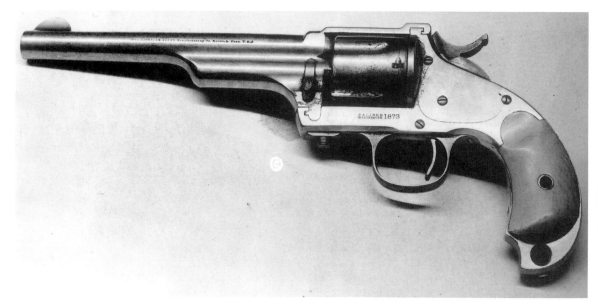

Jesse James's 44 calibre Hopkins and Allen pistol, 1873 model. (Library of Congress, LC-USZ62-50008)

railroad robbery took place in 1873. The bandit gang later expanded to about twenty-six men. In addition to his brother Frank and their cousins, there were Cole Younger and his three brothers, John, James (Jim) and Robert (Bob). Clell Miller, who had served with C. W. Quantrill's guerrilla forces during the war, also joined them.

During those early days following the Civil War, many law-abiding citizens were not too worried when the James gang daringly robbed banks and railroads. Farmers, ranchers and many townspeople, some in desperate economic straits, resented the high charges levied by the banks and railroads. In ensuing years, however, public sympathy waned as a succession of posses, sheriffs and Pinkerton detectives hunted the gang over twelve states and managed to kill eleven of them in various gun-fights.

John Younger was one of the first to be shot, in 1874. The remaining Younger brothers were captured on 7 September 1876, during the failed attempt of the James gang to rob the First National Bank at Northfield, Minnesota. When leaving the bank the gang, eight in number, were met by a hail of gunfire from a group of cit-

izens, who pursued them as they fled into nearby swampland. Only the two James brothers managed to escape. The three Younger brothers were sentenced to long terms of imprisonment and Bob died of tuberculosis in prison. After release, Jim Younger suffered ill-health and put a bullet through his head in 1902. Cole Younger died of a heart attack. It has been estimated that the James gang murdered about thirteen men in their ten-year reign of terror in the Middle West.

By 1882, aged thirty-four, Jesse had curtailed his bandit activities and, as a fugitive from the law, lived under an assumed name, Thomas Howard, with his wife and two children on the outskirts of St Joseph, Missouri. At the time, Governor Crittenden of Missouri offered a $10,000 reward for the capture of Jesse, dead or alive. This proved too great a temptation for two of the outlaw's young confederates, Robert and Charles Ford. On the morning of 3 April 1882, while the Fords were visiting his home, Jesse, unarmed, mounted a chair to straighten a picture. While his back was turned, Robert Ford shot him, killing him instantly.

Shortly afterwards, Jesse's brother Frank surrendered to the authorities and was brought to trial for murder and robbery on two separate occasions, in Missouri and Alabama. He was in

Last gun used by Jesse James, 45 Schofield. (Library of Congress, LC-USZ62-50007)

custody for some time during both trials but was not convicted. Upon release, he took part in a Wild West Show and thereafter lived a law-abiding life. Later he retired and spent his time quietly on the family farm in Missouri, until he died in 1915 at the age of seventy-one, in the room where he was born.

BILL DOOLIN

The American West produced yet another famous outlaw in the shape of Bill Doolin, a former member of the notorious Dalton brothers' band of bank and train robbers. This gang comprised Robert (Bob), Gratton (Grat), William (Bill) and Emmett Dalton, supported by Bill Doolin and several others. The Daltons' older cousins were the Younger brothers. Lewis Dalton, father of the Dalton boys, was a saloon-keeper; after he abandoned his wife Adeline (née Younger), she bravely brought up their fifteen children on her own. The four Dalton boys who became outlaws first worked as cowboys. Another elder brother, Frank, became a federal deputy marshal but was slain by whiskey runners in 1887. After his death, Grat, Bob and Emmett Dalton became lawmen themselves for a short time but drifted into horse-thieving. As a

result, they were forced to leave their law jobs and started to rob stage-coaches, banks and trains. Their other brother Bill then joined them, as did Bill Doolin.

On the morning of 5 October 1892, Doolin's horse went lame and he was unable to ride with the rest of the Dalton gang in their bold attempt to rob two banks at the same time in Coffeyville, Kansas. This mishap possibly saved his life. The venture ended in disaster with Bob and Grat Dalton shot dead, Emmett severely wounded and two others in the gang, Bill Powers and Dick Broadwell, killed. In the same gunfight, Marshal Charles Connelly was also slain, together with three vigilante citizens. The captured Emmett Dalton later served fourteen years in Kansas State Penitentiary in Lansing.

After this débâcle, Doolin formed another outlaw group, which included the remaining Dalton brother, Bill, who had not participated in the Coffeyville robbery. They robbed banks and trains for some three years, mainly from their hideout near Ingalls, in Oklahoma. The gang gained their first sizeable haul during November 1892, when they rode across the border and took about $18,000 by holding up the bank at Spearville, Kansas. A large posse of deputy marshals was then given the task of hunting the bandits. They achieved only partial success when they

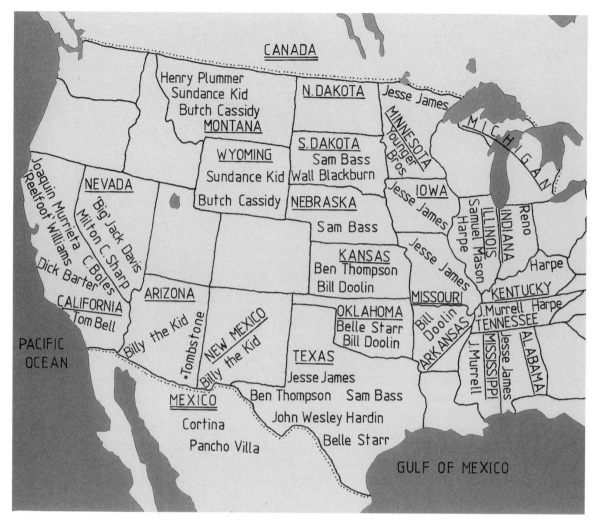

The main states in which major American Western outlaws operated.

ambushed Doolin's desperadoes near their Oklahoma hideout. In the resulting gun-fight, the deputy marshals wounded four of the gang and captured another, but the rest, including Doolin, escaped. The lawmen suffered severe losses themselves, with three of their number killed, in addition to two local bystanders.

After the narrow escape, Doolin led his remaining men across the border into Arkansas. They continued their hold-ups, although their numbers were gradually depleted in various encounters with the law. Bill Dalton also left Doolin's gang to form his own band of outlaws, dying on 8 June 1894 when lawmen crept up behind and shot him

as he was playing with his daughter on the front porch of his home. In the end, only Doolin and a confederate known as 'Little' Dick West remained. Although hiding in Arkansas, Doolin made occasional visits to see his wife and son who had stayed behind in Oklahoma. On one such visit in August 1896, neighbours betrayed him to the law. As Doolin left his house that evening, carrying a rifle, Marshal Heck Thomas, armed with a shotgun, was waiting in the shadow of a tree. The two men fired simultaneously, Doolin's shot missed its target but Marshal Thomas's found its mark and Oklahoma's most famous bandit fell dead.

'BILLY THE KID'

Without doubt the most notorious outlaw of the American South West was 'Billy the Kid', who operated in New Mexico and Arizona. Although he was a ruthless cold-blooded killer and possibly a psychopath, he possessed a certain amount of charisma and played a significant role in the battle of the cattle barons during the so-called Lincoln County cattle war in New Mexico. His real name was William H. Bonney and he was born in New York on the city's east side on 23 November 1859, the son of William and Catherine Bonney. (Some historians think their real surname was McCarty because their son, in his youth, called himself Henry McCarty and only used Bonney in later life.)

Three years after his birth, the family moved to Coffeyville, Kansas where his father died; his mother took her three children to Colorado, married a miner, William Antrim, in 1863, and moved with family first to Sante Fé and then, in 1868, to Silver City, New Mexico. The children were sent to school for a time, but twelve-year-old William was already more fascinated by the local saloons and gambling halls, where in one incident he reputedly stabbed a man to death. His mother died when he was fifteen, and by the age of eighteen he was rumoured to have killed at least another eleven men in various robberies and disputes. He became a cowhand, under the alias of Henry Antrim and he gained the nickname 'Billy the Kid' because of his relative youth and small stature.

In 1877 he became an employee of J. H. Tunstall, who was a representative, along with A. McSween, of John Chisum, the head of a large cattle faction involved in a bloody dispute with another faction headed by L. G. Murphy and J. J. Dolan. The Chisum group grazed some 100,000 head of cattle over land claimed to belong by right to a number of small ranchers and settlers, represented by Murphy and Dolan. Frequent skirmishes between the groups took place from 1876 to 1878. There had always been feuds between cattlemen and sheep-

Billy the Kid. (Library of Congress, LC-USZ62-39572)

men, large landowners and homesteaders, in New Mexico and also in neighbouring Colorado. These occurrences culminated in a savage three-day gunfight which became known as the Lincoln County Cattle War, in which many lost their lives. After John Tunstall was shot by a posse of the rival Murphy faction, 'Billy the Kid' led a band of men in revenge killings. In one incident, the gang killed Sheriff James Brady, together with his deputy and Billy became 'Wanted for Murder'.

After the shoot-out at Lincoln in New Mexico there was a tacit truce. The state governor, General Lew Wallace, offered a provisional amnesty to those who had taken part in the battle provided they were not already under an indictment for another criminal offence. This condition excluded 'Billy the Kid'. Although a pardon was offered to him if he surrendered and was convicted, he refused to give himself up at the end of a parole period. Instead, he joined and later led a

Left: Sheep raid in Colorado. Wood engraving of a Frenzeny drawing in 'Harper's Weekly,' Oct. 13, 1877. (Library of Congress, LC-USZ62-8477)

Right: Sheriff Pat Garrett who pursued and shot 'Billy the Kid' in July 1881. (National Archives, Maryland, USA)

group of twelve men, all wanted for various criminal offences. They went on a rampage of large-scale cattle stealing and killings in the locality of Fort Sumner, in New Mexico.

In 1880, a powerful group of cattlemen, incensed by the rustling, persuaded Patrick Floyd Garrett, a former friend of 'Billy the Kid', to become sheriff of Lincoln County. Pat Garrett had formerly worked as a cowboy and buffalo hunter in Texas, after leaving his home in

Louisiana at the age of seventeen. By 1879 he had married and settled in Lincoln County. Upon his appointment, his immediate task was to break up 'Billy the Kid's' gang. He tracked them for many months and in December 1880 killed one of the group in an ambush at Fort Sumner. The rest escaped but a few days later Billy and three others were trapped and forced to surrender. At his trial in Mesilla, New Mexico during April 1880, 'Billy the Kid' was found guilty of the murder of

Sheriff James Brady and sentenced to hang at Lincoln on 13 May. Although manacled in leg-irons and handcuffs, he managed to escape on 30 April, after killing the two deputies guarding him.

Sheriff Pat Garrett took up his trail again and about ten weeks later traced him to the ranch house of one of his friends, Pete Maxwell, at Fort Sumner. On the night of 14/15 July 1881 Garrett entered the house, leaving two deputies on the porch outside. He found 'Billy the Kid' in a dark-ened bedroom and shot him at point-blank range. One bullet hit the outlaw in the chest and another struck the headboard of the bed. It was claimed that he was holding a gun in his hand at the time but hesitated to use it, perhaps thinking that his friend Pete Maxwell had entered the room. 'Billy the Kid' was twenty-one when he died, which by coincidence was the number of murders he was alleged to have committed in his short lifetime, although this could well have been an exaggeration.

Sheriff Pat Garrett lived on to the age of fifty-seven, when he was shot on 29 February 1908, after a dispute over the lease of his horse ranch to Wayne Brazel. The killing took place on the road from the ranch to Las Cruces. Brazel claimed he shot Garrett in self-defence, after the former sheriff drew a gun on him. There were suspicions that other people might have been involved in a conspiracy to execute the former lawman, with his many enemies. Although he was apparently shot in the back of the head, lack of evidence cleared Brazel.

JOHN WESLEY HARDIN

An outlaw with even more blood on his hands than 'Billy the Kid' was John Wesley Hardin, born in Bonham, Texas in 1853, the son of a travelling Methodist preacher. In 1868, when only fifteen, he killed his first victim, a negro ex-slave, by shooting him with a pistol. By the age of twenty-five, he had killed possibly as many as forty men. Unusually for an American outlaw, most of the murders stemmed from political and racial hatred. It was thought he only used his gun once to obtain money, when

he encountered desperate times in the last year of his life. He was a man of some intellect, studying law while serving a long prison sen-tence and also writing his autobiography, which was published posthumously.

John Wesley Hardin grew up in the aftermath of the Civil War, during the early reconstruction period when the defeated Confederate States of the south were brought back into the Union, after accepting the principle of black citizenship and franchise. Much lawlessness and violence then erupted. The Confederate money previously used in the state was then worthless and the only assets available to Texans were their huge herds of cattle. The big demand for meat in the richer northern states resulted in large-scale cattle drives northward to sell them. Southern eco-nomic depression revived hatred for the Unionist government, together with the new state police force which included both whites and negroes. Many white Texans, including Hardin, consid-ered the new police to be corrupt. A Confederate sympathiser, with strong anti-negro prejudice, he had no qualms when murdering them, or for that matter killing whites who supported the state police force he so despised.

Hardin's prowess with the gun and the murder-ous use to which he put it gained him much local admiration. Although married, with children, he was not cut out for a peaceful domestic life. He frequented saloons, gambled and never backed down in an argument. On 17 May 1873 he saw Jack Helm, a hated former member and captain in the state police force, outside a blacksmith's shop in Albuquerque, Texas. Helm appeared to be intimidating a former political opponent, who happened to be Hardin's friend. Without hesita-tion, Hardin blasted Helm with a shotgun and killed him. This brutal action gained him not only further notoriety but also outright praise from many Texans who had previously suffered at the hands of Jack Helm.

Twelve months later, Hardin visited Comanche in Texas for a horse-race meeting. The deputy sheriff, Charles Webb, thought he would gain some prestige in the town by beating the outlaw to the draw and gunning him down. At first, he pretended to be on sociable terms with the visitor and the pair walked together down the street to the saloon, just before sunset. When Hardin turned his head for a moment, the sheriff took his chance and drew his gun. Instinctively the outlaw jumped sideways, simultaneously reaching for his gun. Although the sheriff fired first, wounding Hardin, the latter's shot, a split second later, struck Webb in the head and killed him. Hardin claimed afterwards he had survived because, like other expert gun-fighters, he had taken his time to ensure his shot hit its target accurately.

The slaying of the deputy sheriff led to a manhunt for the outlaw, who therefore left Texas and went to Alabama and then on to Florida. The previous year the detested state police force in Texas had been abolished and replaced by a force more acceptable to the general public, and meanwhile the Texas Rangers had been reinforced. It was they who eventually tracked Hardin down. A Ranger named J. B. Armstrong obtained permission to travel east to locate the fugitive. In 1877, Armstrong found him, boarded the train on which he was travelling with some cronies, entered his carriage and drew his gun to make the arrest. This time John Wesley Hardin was slow on the draw because his gun became snagged. One of his companions fired at the Texas Ranger but missed and the law officer immediately shot him dead. A physical fight then ensued between Hardin and Armstrong, who was determined take the outlaw back alive. He managed to knock Hardin's weapon aside and then struck him unconscious with his gun. Having disarmed the others, Armstrong escorted Hardin back to Texas to face trial.

He was convicted and eventually served about fifteen years in the state prison. During this long spell, his wife died and upon release in 1892, he renewed contact for a while with his three grown-up children. In 1895, however, Hardin left them for the violent town of El Paso where he was soon leading a degenerate life. He lived with a prostitute and started to rob. On the evening of 18 August of that year he was drinking in a bar when an El Paso policeman, John Selman, shot him in the back. Selman had previously been a professional gunman in Texas, so he might have

done the killing purely to enhance his own image as a gunfighter. Perhaps he also nursed an old grudge against Hardin. Alternatively, as a policeman he may simply have judged the criminal too dangerous to challenge and arrest.

BEN THOMPSON

Another notable Texan gunman and gambler was Benjamin F. Thompson, commonly known as Ben Thompson, who originally came from England. He was born on the 2 November 1843 in Knottingley, Yorkshire. His father was a seafarer and the family emigrated to Texas just before the Civil War. Ben Thompson first worked as a typesetter in Austin, the state capital, but spent much of his time gambling in the saloons. He joined the Confederate army during the war and afterwards served as a mercenary in Mexico. It was rumoured that he shot several of his compatriots in various arguments at about this time. As a result, when he returned to Texas, he arrived with a reputation as a gunman. Ben Thompson had a brother William, commonly called Billy, who was wild, reckless and constantly involved in fights and other trouble. Ben rescued his brother from many tricky situations and in 1868 helped him to escape from Texas after he had killed a man.

Later that same year, Thompson also murdered a man, his brother-in-law, for which crime he served a prison sentence. Upon release in 1870, he drifted to the cow town of Abilene in Kansas, where 'Wild Bill' Hickok was marshal. Ben ran a saloon there with a partner, Phil Coe, until the latter was killed in 1871, in a gun-fight with Hickok. Ben was out of the town at the time, visiting his family. Upon hearing the news, he never returned to Abilene and went to Ellsworth, Kansas where he joined his brother again. He enjoyed gambling with the cattlemen in the saloons there and became popular with them. In 1873, however, the Thompson brothers got into a gambling argument with a man known as 'Happy Jack' Morco. Sheriff Chauncey Whitney, a friend of the Thompsons, intervened to calm the situation down. Unfortunately, Billy was drunk at the time and shot the sheriff with his brother's shotgun. Ben, although upset at the shooting of their friend, protected Billy by holding everyone at bay until his brother was safely out of town. Later, in 1877, the law caught up with Billy Thompson and he was tried for murder. But a combination of circumstances – the passage of four years since the crime, a plea of accidental shooting and a little bribery, so it was rumoured, on Ben's part – brought Billy an acquittal.

Afterwards, Ben Thompson went to Dodge City where he worked as a hired gunman, helping to guard the Sante Fé railroad. He also gambled and later left his job, investing money he had saved in various Texas gambling saloons. Later, he performed the fairly remarkable feat of becoming the elected marshal of Austin, the state capital. However, he was forced to quit the law post in 1882, after involvement in a fatal gun-fight in San Antonio with gambler Jack Harris. In 1884 Ben revisited San Antonio accompanied by another desperado, John King Fisher. Former gambling friends of Harris learned of the visit and ambushed the pair at the Vaudeville Variety Theatre; Ben Thompson and John Fisher both died in a burst of gunfire.

'BUTCH' CASSIDY AND THE 'SUNDANCE KID'

The notorious outlaws 'Butch' Cassidy and the 'Sundance Kid' were still active at the turn of the century, eventually continuing their criminal activities in South America. In 1900, after stealing about $30,000 from the Winnemucca First National Bank in Nevada, they hurriedly left the country to escape the fast-closing net of the law. It was believed that Cassidy fled to England and later to Argentina where he bought a cattle ranch in the west, close to the Chilean border. His confederate, the 'Sundance Kid' and girlfriend Etta Place later joined him in South America and they robbed a few more banks. On one occasion in 1905, they journeyed with Etta to Rio Gallegos in eastern Argentina, having arranged an appointment with the manager of the London and Tarapacá Bank, on the pretext of opening an account. Once inside, the two outlaws overpowered the unsuspecting manager and tied him up, before proceeding to empty the safe. Etta remained outside keeping watch, until the two men came out; then she cut the telegraph line with a shot before the trio escaped.

As already mentioned, the luck of 'Butch' Cassidy and the 'Sundance Kid' finally ran out in 1909 when they were reputedly shot by soldiers of the Bolivian army, at the village of San Vincente. Their bodies, however, were never positively identified and the exact position of their graves still remains unknown. Relatives claimed that both men escaped to settle in San Diego. The true facts will probably never be known.

CHAPTER TEN

BUSHRANGERS –
AUSTRALIAN BRIGANDS

Bushrangers terrorised the Australian outback during three main periods over approximately ninety years, commencing with the convict era, from 1789 onward, through the gold rush period of the 1850s and the Ned Kelly era, culminating in his hanging in 1880. Thereafter the menace of the bushranger gradually decreased as roads, railways, the telegraph and the telephone provided better access to the bush.

In the first period of lawlessness, convicts escaped after suffering the harsh conditions and the brutal floggings meted out in the early prison settlements. Once free, they had little alternative but to rob to survive and most used unwarranted violence towards their victims. During the first half of the nineteenth century, some four-fifths of the population of New South Wales consisted of convicts and ex-convicts, who swelled the criminal ranks. Very few free settlers had arrived since the first penal settlement was founded in 1788 on the shores of Sydney Cove. Most released convicts stayed in the colony, although in theory they were free to return to Britain. In reality, there were few ships to take them and the fare home was beyond the reach of most. Furthermore, about

A battle between mounted police and a bushranger. Picture by George Hamilton, 1875.
(State Library of New South Wales)

twenty-five per cent of all convicts transported to Australia were of Irish stock and they bore hatred towards the mainly Protestant English, not on religious grounds but because of the English land seizures in Ireland. Most of the convicts were former labourers or farm workers and few could read or write. The fact that many had been made convicts unjustly bred instinctive hostility towards the police and the law.

The second and third main periods of bushranging in Australia, the gold rush of the 1850s and the later Ned Kelly era, were the products mainly of greed and the lure of easy riches. Some people took the view that much of the bushranger activity was due to social and economic injustices. Prevailing legislation certainly protected the wealthy, and in the 1860s and 1870s most usable land had been allocated. However, these factors could not justify murder and robbery. In any event, many bushrangers would probably have pursued their criminal ways, even if conditions had been better.

The economy was based on sheep production for Australia's great wool industry, and many mil-

A mail-coach robbery by hooded bushrangers near Mudgee, New South Wales, in 1874. (State Library of New South Wales)

lions of acres of land in New South Wales and Victoria were in the hands of the pasturalists. When the gold-mining industry dwindled, thousands of men competed for too few jobs or to obtain plots of land to start small farms, in order to grow wheat or other crops. The demands to 'unlock the land' to allow a better and fairer distribution became very powerful in the 1860s, and various Land Selection Acts were passed. Some proposed the eviction of squatters to free the large areas of land they had occupied outside the earlier agreed limits of settlement. In the pioneer days, many of

these illegal settlers had driven off the dingoes and the aboriginal tribes from their traditional hunting grounds, resulting in a huge increase in the kangaroo population, as the balance of nature was disturbed. Many squatters later became rich and powerful, privileged at the expense of the rural poor. The turmoil, unrest and corruption of the 1860s produced many bushrangers who were actively supported, sheltered and at times admired by disgruntled 'selectors' or smallholders, who chose to ignore the outlaws' murderous deeds.

THE CONVICT ERA

In Tasmania, known as Van Diemen's Land before 1856, two of the earliest, most violent and probably deranged bushrangers were John Whitehead and Michael Howe. The former operated from 1810 to 1815 and the latter from 1814 to 1818. Whitehead arrived in Tasmania after being given a life transportation sentence at York Assizes for stealing two pairs of breeches. After escaping, he led a notorious gang of twenty-eight bushrangers, including Howe as his second-in-command. The gang robbed and terrorised settlers on both sides of the Derwent River in the south and centre of the colony. Whitehead imposed ruthless discipline on his men and allegedly punished one of them by filling his footwear with bull ants, before forcing his feet into them and leaving him bound helpless to die in agony. Eventually, the military tracked down the gang and Whitehead was shot. Just before he died and before the soldiers could reach him, he asked Howe to cut off his head and hide it, so that the military could not claim the reward on offer for his capture. Before escaping, Howe complied with his request and afterwards became leader of the remainder of the gang.

Howe, later nicknamed 'Black Howe', was born in Yorkshire in 1787 and was transported to Tasmania in 1812 for seven years for committing highway robbery, a relatively minor sentence compared to that of his confederate John Whitehead. He escaped in 1814 when he joined Whitehead's gang. After later becoming leader, he planned robberies with military precision and,

STICKING
MUD...

similarly to his predecessor, imposed harsh discipline on gang members. In 1817, the many successful raids on settlements resulted in the Lieutenant-Governor of Tasmania, William Sorell, offering him an amnesty for his many crimes, on condition he surrendered and gave information on other bushrangers. Howe refused the offer, boasting that he preferred to remain the true 'lieutenant-governor of the ranges' while Sorell controlled only the towns. Howe survived another year in the bush but lost many of his men who were either killed or captured. Eventually, in 1818, an agent infiltrated the gang and clubbed him to death, near his hut at Shannon River.

Although the vast majority of bushrangers were convicts transported from England, two native Australians, the Aboriginals Musquito and Tegg, joined the ranks. Musquito, skilled in the art of bush survival, evaded capture in Tasmania for several years until 1825 when he was tracked down by Tegg. The reward on offer for his capture was not paid, probably because Tegg was an Aborigine; the Aborigines in Tasmania were scornfully and brutally treated by those who had occupied their homeland. As a result, the disillusioned Tegg took to the bush himself.

A particularly violent bushranger was Alexander Pierce (or Pearce) who escaped from the Macquarie Harbour penal settlement in western Tasmania with eight fellow prisoners and later became a cannibal. In contrast, Martin Cash and Matthew Brady were both noted for the humane treatment of their victims.

Cash was born in Enniscorthy, County Wexford, Ireland in 1808 and was transported to New South Wales in 1827 for seven years as an assigned servant. After serving his sentence for housebreaking, he engaged in cattle 'duffing', an Australian slang term for livestock stealing. To avoid arrest he left for Tasmania where later, in 1839, he was captured, convicted of larceny and imprisoned. In 1842, he escaped with two others by swimming away from the Port Arthur penal settlement and the following year became leader of a bushranger gang known as 'Cash and Co'. He earned the nickname 'Gentleman Matt' Cash because of his courteous manner towards his vic-

tims. After two years in the bush he was captured in Hobart and served another long sentence at Norfolk Island, a prison settlement about 300 miles off the coast of Sydney, until he gained a pardon for good behaviour. He then spent several years in New Zealand before returning to Tasmania where later he became the head of the Hobart Botanical Gardens. Martin Cash thus became a respected figure, noted for always wearing a top hat, who died in 1877.

Brady, born in 1799, was sent to Tasmania for insubordination, after first being transported to New South Wales for forgery in 1820. He later gained the reputation of being particularly charming to ladies and only using violence in self-defence. His many daring attacks on property commenced in 1824, after escaping with six other prisoners, from Macquarie Harbour. They stole a boat and sailed it along the coast to the mouth of the Derwent River. They landed and survived in the bush for two years, with the help of sympathisers, and on one occasion managed to release all the prisoners held in Sorell gaol, after first capturing the township. Brady also cheekily offered a reward for the Lieutenant-Governor's capture. Brady was eventually caught in 1826 and despite pleas for leniency, the bushranger went to the gallows at the age of twenty-seven.

On mainland Australia, many bushrangers were quick to emulate the first convict to escape, former slave John Caesar, who was killed by a settler in 1796 at Liberty Plains, Sydney. One of the most famous early outlaws was John Donahoe, born in 1806 in Dublin, Ireland, convicted in 1823 of 'intent to commit a felony' and transported to Sydney. He worked as an assigned servant until he took to the bush in 1827 with two confederates. They ambushed bullock carts along the Windsor Road, outside Sydney, but were swiftly apprehended and sentenced to death. Donahoe managed to escape and for the next two years robbed with another gang around the Sydney area and the Penrith and Campbelltown districts of New South Wales. His main accomplice was 'Darkey' Underwood who later formed his own gang. In 1830, mounted troopers finally tracked down Donahoe near Campbelltown and, after he taunted them to fire, shot him dead. Afterwards, he gained fame because of his brave defiance of authority and the sympathy he had often shown for emancipists – ex-convicts, most of them poor, who had served their terms. His exploits became the subject of 'The Wild Colonial Boy' ballads. He also featured as the hero in the bush folksong 'Bold Jack Donahoe', which became so popular that its singing was once banned in public bars. As a further indication of his fame, men proudly smoked pipes with their bowls fashioned in the shape of the bushranger's death mask.

If Donahoe had not been shot dead, he could well have met his fate at the hands of the official executioner Alexander Green, who presided at Sydney from 1828 to 1855. He was himself a former minor criminal, having been transported for life for stealing a piece of cloth from a shop in Shropshire in 1824. He received a conditional pardon a year later and gained employment as one of the official 'floggers' in the colony of New South Wales. He became a hated figure and especially so when he gained promotion to executioner. On one occasion in 1830, a young bushranger named Thomas Tiernan, with the rope already around his neck, attacked him. He threw the executioner from the scaffold to the ground several feet below, breaking his arm. At the same time Tiernan also fell off the gallows' platform, strangling himself on the end of the rope. Despite his fractured limb, Green climbed back on to the scaffold, pulled the youth back and proceeded with the official execution, hanging him by the drop through the trapdoor.

A popular bushranger who succeeded Jack Donahoe was Edward Davis, known as 'Teddy the Jew-boy', who robbed with his gang in the Hunter River Valley district of New South Wales from 1839 to 1840. A transported convict, he was popular for his humane treatment of victims and his sense of dry humour. He was even said to have given some of his booty to the poor on several occasions. The authorities captured his gang in 1840 and all were hanged together in February 1841, despite many calls for Davis to receive

Major centres of bushranging in nineteenth-century Australia.

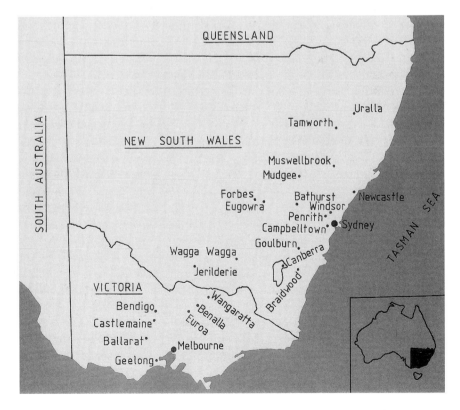

Armed bushranger chased by police. Pencil sketch by Samuel Calvert, 1861.
(State Library of New South Wales)

clemency. In complete contrast, the ruthless murderer John Lynch roamed the bush from 1840 to 1841. An ex-convict, he killed at least nine people with an axe before he was caught in 1841. He then confessed to his crimes and was hanged at the age of nineteen.

THE GOLD RUSH ERA
AND LATER PERIOD

In the 1860s the best-known bushrangers in New South Wales were Frank Gardiner, Ben Hall and John Gilbert, who sometimes worked together. Although they commanded some public sympathy, being Australian-born rather than transported convicts, they still struck terror in the hearts of many families living on remote sheep and cattle stations far away from police protection. The many failures to capture them eventually resulted in the reorganisation of the New South Wales police force.

Gardiner was probably born around 1830 at Boro Creek, now in the Australian Capital Territory south of Goulburn, although he once claimed

he was born in Scotland and that his real name was Christie. The latter was true, for he was the son of a Scottish free settler named Christie and a half-caste Irish Aboriginal servant girl. He only assumed the name Frank Gardiner in about 1860, modelling his criminal life along the lines of an English highwayman. In 1850, the police arrested him for horse-theft in Victoria and he received a five-year prison sentence. He served only a few months before escaping and fleeing to New South Wales. In 1854, Gardiner was again arrested for horse-stealing and this time sentenced to fourteen years on Cockatoo Island in Sydney Harbour. After five years, he managed to gain release on a 'ticket of leave' and apparently worked honestly as a butcher for a time. However, in 1861, he was charged with cattle-stealing but eluded the law and became a bushranger, working at first with John Piesley, who had also served a sentence on Cockatoo Island. They moved to the goldfields at Lambing Flat in New South Wales and committed several highway robberies. Piesley was later captured and hanged in

1862. Gardiner then formed a larger gang and Gilbert became his second-in-command. The latter was born in Canada and, after arriving in Australia, mixed with many unsavoury characters and small-time thieves.

In 1862, Gardiner and his men ambushed and robbed the Eugowra gold escort in New South Wales of about 28,000 Australian dollars, in gold dust and notes. Although a few of the gang were later arrested and some of the money recovered, Gardiner escaped the law and went to the Apis Creek goldfield, near Rockhampton in Queensland, where he became a shopkeeper and hotelier.

Gilbert remained in New South Wales and became second-in-command to Ben Hall, who took over the remnants of Gardiner's gang. Gilbert was often generous with his ill-gotten gains; for example, in 1863, in a hotel in Carcoar, New South Wales, he bought poor people free drinks, threw cigars on the tables and provided food for them. The following year, the police traced his former leader, Gardiner, to Queensland and arrested him; his whereabouts had accidently been revealed by Gardiner's companion Kitty Brown, when she wrote a letter to relatives. The judge sentenced Gardiner to thirty-two years' imprisonment, with hard labour. He set-

Frank Gardiner, bushranger, after ten years in Darling-hurst Gaol. 'Illustrated Sydney News', 30 August, 1890. (State Library of New South Wales)

tled down to become a model prisoner and after ten years in Darlinghurst gaol received a pardon, on condition he left Australia. This controversial decision brought down the government of Sir Henry Parkes in New South Wales. Gardiner departed to China and later arrived in the United States of America where he kept a saloon. The rest of his life remains unknown, although it was rumoured he died in the 1890s when he would have been in his sixties, an unusually long life for a bushranger.

Ben Hall, who took over Frank Gardiner's gang in 1862, was born in 1837 at Breeza, near Tamworth in New South Wales. His father moved to Murrurundi, also in New South Wales, to farm and Ben attended school there. Later his father moved again to a station near Forbes, in the same colony, and Ben became a stockman. He married an Irish lass when he was nineteen years old and the cou-

ple had two children. Hall appeared contented to farm with cattle and horses until his wife left him. Shortly afterwards, in 1862, the police charged him with armed highway robbery but he was released on lack of evidence. Later in the year they accused him of having taken part in the earlier Eugowra gold escort robbery with Frank Gardiner but again he was not convicted. Upon returning to his farm, he found most of his stock had strayed and after an encounter with the police in which shots were fired, he took to the bush.

After becoming the leader of Frank Gardiner's old gang, he unleashed a three-year reign of terror and during this period committed over sixty robberies. Hall's gang comprised his right-hand man John Gilbert and three others. Their crimes included about ten mail robberies, twenty raids on settlers' homes, attacks on country stores and

Ben Hall, bushranger. 'Illustrated Melbourne Post', 22 May 1865. (State Library of New South Wales)

several bank and gold escort hold-ups. They armed themselves well and often rode stolen racehorses to ensure swift getaways. Although Hall gained the reputation of occasionally showing chivalry towards his victims, whom he rarely killed, he humiliated any policeman he temporarily held captive. In 1863, he and his men raided the homestead of Henry Keightley, a police magistrate, at Dunn's Plains, about thirty miles from Bathurst. During the mêlée, Keightley shot one of the gang, Michael Burke. In retaliation, another member wanted to kill the magistrate but Hall intervened, telling Keightley his life would be spared if he paid a ransom, equivalent to the reward on offer for the man he had just shot. Hall allowed the magistrate's wife to travel to Bathurst to collect the money and she returned, within the time set by the outlaw, to save her husband's life.

In 1863, the bushranger attacked a sheep station near Forbes, setting fire to the barn in the process. During the raid, a further member of his gang was killed, with another surrendering shortly afterwards. Hall and Gilbert then parted company for about six months before joining forces again with a new recruit, John Dunn. The trio carried out many robberies along the road from Sydney to Melbourne. In November 1864, they made plans to rob the mail-coach as it travelled along the road near Jugiong, New South Wales. Before its arrival, the three bushrangers blocked the road and forcibly detained and robbed some sixty travellers, subsequently capturing a solitary policeman who was kept with the rest of the captives by the roadside, guarded by one of the bushrangers. When the mail-coach approached, it was escorted by a constable and two other police officers, including a sergeant named Parry. In the ensuing fight, Gilbert killed Sergeant Parry and the other police officers surrendered. The bushrangers then took their plunder from the mail-coach, watched by the captive bystanders. A few months later, Hall and his two accomplices rode into the village of Collector to rob the hotel. Dunn remained on guard outside, while the other two went inside. A police constable named Nelson, the father of eight children, arrived on the scene and Dunn callously shot him dead, allowing the gang to escape.

Although Hall had not personally killed, he was an accessory to the murders of both Sergeant Parry and Constable Nelson. This somewhat

The shooting of Sergeant Parry by John Gilbert during the mail-coach robbery near Jugiong, New South Wales, in 1864. (State Library of New South Wales)

destroyed the image of chivalry bestowed upon him by some of the bush population. A determined effort was made to capture him and early in May 1865 a police patrol of six men and two Aboriginal trackers set off to find him, one of whom was Billy Dargin, one of Hall's former friends. On 5 May 1865, the police discovered the outlaw's hideout at Billabong Creek, near Forbes. He tried to escape but was shot dead by Dargin. Later in the month, the police shot Gilbert at the home of Thomas Kelly, Dunn's grandfather, who may have betrayed him. Dunn escaped and retained his freedom until the following year, when he was captured and hanged on 19 March 1866.

In contrast to the trio of Hall, Gilbert and Dunn, bushranger Daniel Morgan always worked alone. He was an evil, ruthless and probably insane killer and thus became known variously as 'Mad' Morgan, 'Mad Dog' Morgan and 'Black' Dan Morgan. He was later also called the 'Terror of the Murrumbidgee', as he operated in the region of that river in New South Wales. He was probably born at Campbelltown, New South Wales, in about 1830, the son of a costermonger who sold cabbages, known as 'Gypsy' Fuller, and a prostitute called Kate Owen. The surname used by their son may have been inspired by that of the pirate Henry Morgan, who wreaked havoc across the Spanish Main in the seventeenth century.

Morgan committed his first known offence in 1854 when he robbed a hawker near Castlemaine in Victoria. He was apprehended and sentenced to twelve years' hard labour but gained an early release in 1860. He went to work as a stockman in the Riverina region of New South Wales but became a bushranger in 1862. He carried out many robberies and several murders, including that of a police trooper. He was thought to revel in killing, as he shot men when they posed no threat, when unarmed or asleep. In 1864 the authorities offered a large reward for his capture and he left for Victoria where he continued to rob travellers, terrorise stations and burn down farm buildings. In 1865 he raided the Peechelba station, near Wangaratta, and held the occupants hostage. While inside the house, he spotted a child crying outside and in a strange momentary change of character allowed a servant, Alice Mac-Donald, to go and tend the infant. This unusual act of kindness brought about Morgan's downfall, as the servant ran away to inform the police. Shortly afterwards, they arrived at the station, reinforced by several stockmen who had offered their assistance. The outlaw attempted to escape but was shot dead, as he mounted his horse, by a stockman named Quinlan. He died on 9 April 1865 at about the age of thirty-five. Later Morgan's head was severed and retained for scientific study.

Morgan, Hall and Gilbert all died in 1865, and for the next couple of years the young Clarke brothers, of convict parentage, took their place spreading terror among settlers in the wild mountainous and forested country around Araluen, near Braidwood, New South Wales. The campaign of crime started after Thomas Clarke escaped from Braidwood gaol in 1865, while serving a sentence for robbery. In the space of a few months he waylaid many travellers, stole racehorses, killed a policeman and robbed stores. In the following year, his youngest brother John decided to assist him and together they began holding up mail-coaches. The third brother, James, was unable to join them as he was already in prison, but the two bushranging Clarke brothers later recruited other men to join their criminal enterprise.

In December 1866, a group of four special police constables were sworn-in to track down the Clarke brothers' gang. They were selected because of their intimate knowledge of the terrain where the outlaws operated. The police went undercover, pretending to be land surveyors, and tried to get on friendly terms with the mother and sisters of the Clarke brothers who lived in the area. The families were not deceived and on 5 January 1867, the four policemen were found murdered. It was later revealed that Thomas Clarke had killed three of them and another member of the gang had killed the fourth. Immediately, a large reward was offered for the capture of the Clarkes who, undeterred, carried out further mail-coach robberies. Their luck finally

*Dan Morgan, bushranger, holding up a work party of navvies and burning their tents.
'Illustrated Melbourne Post'. 25 January 1865. (State Library of New South Wales)*

ran out on 27 April 1867, when they were tracked to their hideout in the Jindera Ranges, New South Wales. Troopers surrounded them and after a shooting match the teen-aged Clarke brothers surrendered; they were both hanged on 25 June 1867.

Bushranger Frederick Ward, who called himself 'Captain Thunderbolt', survived for a longer period than the Clarke brothers in New South Wales. Many attributed his success to his great riding skill which enabled him to elude the inadequate police force. He robbed between 1863 and 1868 and gained a reputation, probably erroneously, for his courteous manner towards his victims, especially those of the female sex. He was born in 1835 in the Windsor district of New South Wales and early in his life worked as a horse-breaker and station-hand in the Muswell-

brook and Mudgee districts. In 1856, he was sent to Cuckatoo Island prison for horse-stealing, from where he escaped in 1863 with another prisoner, Frederick Brittain. He took to the bush and operated mainly along the road leading northwards from Newcastle, New South Wales to the Queensland border. He usually worked alone and married a part-Aboriginal, known as 'Yellow Long', who supported him throughout his villainous life in the bush. She later contracted pneumonia and he took her to a settler's home, so that she could die peacefully in relatively comfortable surroundings. In contrast, 'Captain Thunderbolt' died violently when he was shot at Uralla, New South Wales on 25 May 1870.

The use of the assumed title 'Captain' became popular, too, with bushrangers in Victoria. 'Captain Melville', who enjoyed brief notoriety, was former Tasmanian convict Frank McCallum. He had been transported as a youth in 1838 and after gaining his release, took up bushranging in 1852. In December of that year, he visited Geelong and the police recognised and pursued him. 'Captain Melville' attempted to escape by stealing a horse but the owner of the steed intervened and detained him. McCallum was sentenced to thirty-two years for the attempted theft and was incarcerated in the prison hulks, moored in Hobson's Bay. Four years later, in 1856, McCallum and a party of other convicts were being taken by boat to work in a nearby quarry when the prisoners attacked the two guards, overpowered one and murdered the corporal-in-charge. The convicts rowed furiously across the bay to escape but were retaken shortly afterwards. The authorities sentenced McCallum to death but later a reprieve was granted and a very long prison sentence substituted. During July 1857, the bushranger attacked the governor of Melbourne gaol. The following month, McCallum was found dead in his cell; it was reported he had committed suicide.

Andrew George Scott worked under the alias of 'Captain Moonlight' or 'Captain Moonlite'. He was one of the very few well-educated bushrangers and he committed robberies first in Victoria and then in New South Wales. He was born in 1842 in Tyrone, Ireland, the son of a church minister, and he became a qualified engineer. After arriving in Victoria in 1860, he joined the army to serve during the Maori Wars in New Zealand. Upon returning to Victoria, having been wounded in the leg, he took up training to enter the church, but in 1869 commenced his criminal career. In his first masked robbery, he stole a considerable amount of cash and gold from the Mount Egerton bank and forced the manager, before tying him up, to write a note stating that 'Captain Moonlight' had visited and robbed the bank; this was left as his calling card. Scott later bought a yacht in Sydney with a forged cheque but was apprehended and sent to prison for eighteen months. Shortly after release, he was arrested for the earlier Mount Egerton bank robbery, after a gold ingot he sold was identified as one of those stolen from it. He served eight years for this crime

before earning an early release in 1879 for good behaviour, having officiated over the prison's Bible classes.

Scott then worked for a short time as an open-air preacher before gathering together a gang of bushrangers, one of whom was only fifteen years old. They carried out several robberies and late in 1879 raided the Wantabadgery station in the Riverina region, near Wagga Wagga, New South Wales. They captured all the occupants, holding over fifty people hostage, and spent a relaxed weekend there. However, one station-hand managed to escape, riding the twenty-four miles to Wagga Wagga to alert the police. When they arrived, a fierce gun battle took place just outside the station house, which resulted in the death of two of the bushrangers, including the boy. One policeman was shot by Scott, who shortly afterwards surrendered with the remnants of his gang. Upon conviction, Andrew George Scott, alias 'Captain Moonlight', and another of the bushrangers were hanged in January 1880; two others received life imprisonment.

THE NED KELLY ERA

A bushranger named Harry Power, who robbed in Victoria and New South Wales, became well known, not for daring deeds but for the fact that a young lad, Edward (Ned) Kelly, once worked for him. Power was born in 1819 in Waterford, Ireland, and was transported to Tasmania, in 1840, for bank robbery. He avoided serving his seven-year sentence by escaping and then travelling across the sea to Victoria where he became a horse thief. In 1855, he got involved in a fight with some troopers, one of whom he injured badly. As a consequence, Power was charged with wounding with intent and sentenced to fourteen years' imprisonment. For some unknown reason, when he was in the final year of his long prison sentence at Pentridge, Melbourne, he escaped and took to the bush. He then committed robberies in parts of southern New South Wales and in north-eastern Victoria, where he became associated with the Kelly family. The Kellys often feuded with their neighbours and relatives, the Lloyd family; and it was possibly because of Harry Power's friendship with his rivals that Jack Lloyd, who was Ned Kelly's uncle, betrayed Power to the police for a £500 reward. Power was captured near his hideout in King River Valley, Victoria in May 1870. He was sentenced to fifteen years' imprisonment and served the whole term. After his release in 1885, little is known of his life.

During Harry Power's long term of imprisonment, his young former apprentice in crime, Ned Kelly, came to the fore. Edward Kelly was born in 1855, at Beveridge, near Wallan Wallan, about thirty miles north of Melbourne, Victoria. One of three sons and five daughters born to his Irish mother, Ellen (née Quinn), after her marriage to Irish ex-convict John 'Red' Kelly, he attended the local school. When the father died in 1866, the family were left in extreme poverty and moved to Benalla, a remote spot near Glenrowan, in northeast Victoria, where they lived in a shack. In the meantime members of the Lloyd family had married sisters of Ned's mother, Ellen.

From an early age the Kelly brothers, Ned and Daniel, had various tussles with the law, mainly on charges of cattle- and horse-stealing, serving several short prison sentences. Ned also fancied himself as a boxer and on 8 August 1874 won an epic twenty-round bare-knuckle victory over his opponent 'Wild' Wright. Serious trouble erupted, however, in April 1878, when Ned was accused of wounding a policeman named Fitzpatrick, who was attempting to arrest his brother Dan for horse-stealing. The entire Kelly family resisted the attempted arrest, claiming later that it was Dan who had injured the policeman and that Ned had not even been around at the time. The police then charged Mrs Kelly and two neighbours, who were also present, of being accessories to the attempted murder of a police constable. After the court found them guilty, Mrs Kelly served three years in prison and her neighbours six years. Ned and Dan, meanwhile, had fled before they could be arrested and became bushrangers. They were proclaimed outlaws by the Victorian Parliament, using the Felons Apprehension Act of 1878.

Ned Kelly was then twenty-three years old and his brother Dan seventeen. The pair were joined by Steve Hart, an ex-jockey aged eighteen, and Joe Byrne, aged twenty-one; Ned Kelly became leader of the gang. Byrne, born in 1857 at Beechworth, Victoria, was the son of a gold prospector and proved to be Ned Kelly's closest friend and ally. The four desperadoes unleashed a reign of terror along the borderland of Victoria and New South Wales and vented much anger against the detested police.

In October 1878, Ned spotted a four-strong police patrol searching for them in the Wombat Ranges, at Stringybark Creek, near the gang's hide-out. He decided to ambush them. When the police, who were not in uniform, separated into pairs, the Kelly gang attacked. In the ensuing fight, Ned shot dead Constable Lonigan; and his companion, Constable McIntyre, surrendered. When the other two police officers, Sergeant Kennedy and Constable Scanlon, returned to the scene, Ned shot and killed both of them. Constable McIntyre, however, later escaped on Sergeant Kennedy's horse and rode to Mansfield with the news of the killings. The slaughter of the police triggered a huge effort to capture the Kelly gang. A reward of £8000, a huge sum in those days, was offered for their arrest. In addition, the authorities spent well over £100,000 pursuing them, using a specially drafted police force of some 200 men, as well as secret agents.

Despite their cold-blooded brutality, the Kelly gang still retained local support because of their hatred of authority. Several members of the sparse, deprived rural community gave the bushrangers food and protected them from the police by use of the bush telegraph. One man in particular who helped them was Aaron Sherritt, an old schoolboy friend of Byrne. During the next few months, the Kelly gang carried out two daring bank robberies at Euroa, Victoria and Jerilderie, New South Wales. The impudence of these raids, described in Chapter Two, spurred the police into even greater activity and the gang went into hiding. Even though Aaron Sherritt accepted a police bribe for assistance, they survived for over a year; and when Byrne discovered that his former friend had turned traitor, he murdered him in his home, despite his being under police protection. Dan Kelly accompanied Byrne on the murderous mission.

The days of the Kelly gang, nevertheless, were numbered. In June 1880 Byrne and Dan rode to Glenrowan, near Benalla, in the heart of so-called Kelly country, to join Ned and Hart after the shooting of Sherritt. The reunited gang then detained most of the inhabitants of the small settlement in the local hotel. Ned guessed that the police would soon track them to Glenrowan and bring in reinforcements by rail, instead of venturing on the long horseback ride across country. In a murderous plot to kill as many policemen as possible, the Kelly gang removed a section of the railway line on an embankment near Glenrowan, in order to derail the train, before returning to the local hotel bar to await and celebrate the anticipated bloody event. However, the contrived plan misfired, due to the courage of the local schoolmaster who escaped from the hotel after hearing the bushrangers bragging of their plot. He rode to the spot and waved frantically with a red scarf and candle to halt the train. Then he informed the police where the Kelly gang were hiding and holding their hostages.

The police surrounded the wooden shanty of a hotel and a fierce gun battle took place which lasted for many hours. When dawn broke, the police observed a figure clad in armour – who later proved to be Ned Kelly – emerging from the mist. After the police hit him several times with shots, the outlaw fell seriously wounded and was seized. Meanwhile, the battle with the other bushrangers continued, with many of the terri-

WEIGHT
97 pounds

1 2 3 4 5 6

A sketch of the armour worn by Ned Kelly during his futile attempt to escape from the police at Glenrowan. (State Library of New South Wales)

fied hostages lying on the floor to escape the barrage of bullets. When a lull in the shooting occurred, the hostages managed to escape from the building. They reported that only one of their companions remained alive inside and he was fatally wounded; three of the escaped hostages were also wounded and one of them, a child, died later. Joe Byrne had been shot dead but the two other bushrangers, Dan Kelly and Steve Hart, were still alive inside the building.

The police took the decision to burn the building down by tossing in an ignited bundle of straw soaked in kerosene. The wooden building immediately caught fire and when the ensuing blazing inferno subsided, a local Roman Catholic priest volunteered to enter the ruins of the building alone. He came out and reported that no one remained alive and the bodies inside were badly charred by the fire. The only bushranger who still remained alive was the captured Ned Kelly. Why he had earlier left the building clad in armour remained unclear. It might have been a show of bravado but the most probable explanation was that he was trying to escape and save his own skin. Nothing, however, could save him after his conviction for murder on 28 October 1880, and he was hanged in Melbourne on 11 November, even though 32,000 people petitioned for a reprieve. It was reported that before he met the hangman, his mother fortified him with the words, 'Mind you die like a Kelly, Ned.' Mrs Kelly herself lived to the grand old age of ninety-two and died in 1923.

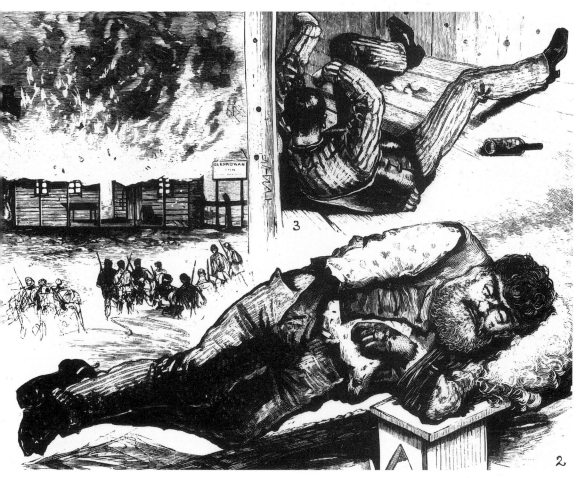

The destruction of Ned Kelly's gang at Glenrowan, Victoria in June 1880.
(State Library of New South Wales)

CHAPTER ELEVEN

MYTHS, FOLKLORE AND ROBIN HOOD

The death of a famous highwayman, outlaw, bushranger or bandit in any part of the world, was usually swiftly followed by myths and folklore in praise of their bravery and daring exploits. Most of these legends were grossly exaggerated but with the passage of time it often became difficult to distinguish between fact and fiction. In real life, however, virtually all these villains lacked the glamour attributed to them and many led sordid and often brutal lives. They carried out their murderous deeds solely to steal and many had become outlaws because they were already in fear of the gallows for previous crimes. A few claimed they robbed for revenge because of some wrong, often imaginary, done to them by society. Because of social injustice and the appalling lot of the poor, the possession of wealth was envied. Sometimes the bandits falsely represented an heroic symbol of revolt to many honest and deprived people, thereby gaining their admiration, sympathy and covert support.

Any outlaw with a hint of a noble origin or a mysterious foreign background always captured the public's imagination, as did the title of 'Captain'. The latter was even applied to villains who never existed, such as the hero of *The Beggar's Opera* by John Gay, which had its première in 1728. This well-known ballad opera successfully combined a satire on the corrupt politics of the day and the moral degradation of society in London, with a parody on Italian opera. In addition, the work possessed all the necessary ingredients to excite the public's imagination. The debonair highwayman 'Captain' Macheath toyed unscrupulously with the affections of two girls, Polly Peachum, whom he secretly married, and Lucy Lockit. Polly's father was a receiver of stolen goods and patron of the highwayman, but when he heard of his daughter's secret marriage, he betrayed Captain Macheath as a robber and he was sent to Newgate Prison. Lucy, the daughter of a gaoler at the prison, loved the highwayman and promised to help him escape; in return, he promised to marry her. When his wife Polly later visited him in prison, he rejected and disowned her in front of Lucy Lockit. However, his wife vowed to remain faithful to him, in spite of his disloyalty and unkind words.

In due course, 'Captain' Macheath escaped, assisted by the gaoler's daughter, but was recaptured shortly afterwards. The authorities sentenced him to death, despite the two girls unavailingly beseeching their fathers to use any influence they had to have their lover pardoned. Macheath calmly accepted his fate, pondering philosophically that rich men can escape the gallows but poor men must always die. However, a mob gathered to petition for the highwayman's release, demanding that the views of the poor should be taken into consideration, as well as those of the powerful. By their action, the 'Captain' was eventually saved from the gallows and returned to his faithful wife Polly, to give the opera a happy finale. A painting by Hogarth of *Captain Macheath* hangs in the Tate Gallery, London. It shows the highwayman wearing leg-irons.

Another fictitious highwayman hero was 'Captain Starlight', created by Thomas Alexander Browne, writing under the pen-name of 'Rolf Boldrewood', in his Australian novel *Robbery Under Arms*. This mysterious aristocrat turned outlaw was a composite bushranger figure, although many incidents in the book have historical foundations. The character was a blend of several real individuals, including 'Captain Moonlight', a gentleman horse thief named 'Midnight', a member of Ben Hall's bushranger gang and several others, such as Harry Redford, who was once involved in a long cattle drive from Queensland to South Australia.

As for Australia's real-life folk hero Ned Kelly, some people obviously thought he was right to defy police authority, even though they knew him to be a cold-blooded killer. This was in some respects analogous to the situation in nineteenth-century England, where for quite different reasons poor country folk would never betray the local village poacher, ignoring the crime because they detested even more the arrogance and power of the landowners. The myths associated with the cult of the bushranger in Australia became well publicised in novels, ballads, films and plays. Ned Kelly's name even entered colloquial language to typify a form of reckless fortitude, with the expression 'as game as Ned Kelly'. The paintings of Sidney Nolan in the twentieth century also helped to immortalise the bushranger.

Even in the seventeenth century, the public were fascinated by the lives of notorious robbers. In 1611, the Jacobean playwrights Middleton and Dekker wrote *The Roaring Girl*, based on the life of 'Moll Cutpurse', the famous lady pickpocket and highwaywoman. When the play was written, she was about twenty-seven years old and therefore in the early days of her long criminal career. As in real life, the play depicted her as a tomboy who was not shy in challenging her male counterparts to sword duels, among other daring escapades that bore some element of truth.

Highwaymen in particular were treated kindly by writers, as if they were a superior class to other types of criminals – a view hardly shared by their victims. 'The Highwayman', a well-known ballad by the English poet Alfred Noyes, published in 1906, depicted the dashing carefree lover who risked capture and the gallows to keep his rendezvous with a maiden, 'the landlord's black-eyed daughter'. The king's men awaited his arrival at the inn, after a robbery on a stormy

An exaggerated fictional view of Jesse James. Such portrayals helped to create the folklore about the outlaw. (Library of Congress, LC-USZ62-2174)

night, his beloved already detained by the waiting men inside. As the highwayman came 'riding-riding-riding' up to the old inn door, the poem assumed an air of suspense and a pronounced rhythm suggestive of hoof-beats. In a vain attempt to warn her lover, the innkeeper's daughter committed suicide before the waiting men shot the highwayman.

Similarly, in France, the dashing exploits of the popular bandit folk hero Louis Dominique Cartouche were dramatised in several plays, ballads and films. Prints and portraits of Cartouche also became extremely popular.

In Britain, a glamorised version of the life of Dick Turpin, published in 1834, launched William Harrison Ainsworth on his career as a successful novelist. Many others before and after him also helped to immortalise the highwayman. A significant element was the creation of the indomitable but fictional horse 'Black Bess', which Dick Turpin supposedly rode to York. The highwayman rode the gallant beast until it dropped dead with exhaustion, when just in sight of the city. Such stories made Turpin a popular legend after his death, depicting him as courteous and considerate, instead of the cruel villain he was in real life. The Victorians also made him a hero, along with others such as Jack Sheppard, in the 'Penny Dreadfuls' published by Edward Lloyd during the 1830s and 1840s. These were serialised in weekly one-penny parts which glamorised, with much imagination, the sensational stories of criminals

A fictionalised view of the death of 'Billy the Kid'. Illustration from an article entitled 'Dandy Rock, the man from Texas.' The Finale – the 'Kid' killed by the sheriff at Fort Sumner. Woodcut from Beadle's half-dime library, vol. 6, 1879. (Library of Congress, LC-USZ62-38981)

and their violent deeds. They sold readily to a public who craved excitement to enliven their relatively dull everyday lives. The 'Penny Dreadfuls' were condemned at the time because of their gruesome nature and potentially bad moral influence, rather as the excessive violence shown on television and in films is criticised today.

Likewise, in the eastern United States of America, during the late nineteenth century, the public possessed a large appetite for blood-and-thunder fiction, especially that of the pioneering West. To satisfy the demand, Edward Zane Carroll Judson, writing under his pen-name of Ned Buntline, travelled widely in the West to obtain background material for his 'Dime Novels', which romanticised the many gun-fights that took place and gave notoriety to many of the participants. Other writers in the 1920s and 1930s, such as Walter Noble Burns and Stuart N. Lake, helped to create the legend of Wyatt Earp by making him a hero as a frontier marshal. Other writers took an opposing view and portrayed the Earp brothers as a close-knit family of itinerant gamblers who sometimes worked as law officers when it suited them to do so, as did their friend 'Doc' Holliday.

'Bat' Masterson became a hero of Western folklore and many exaggerated legends were told about the exploits of 'Wild Bill' Hickok and 'Buffalo Bill'. The latter helped to dramatise the Wild West in his hugely successful show, with a cast of 800 cowboys and Indians, which toured America, Europe and Britain. It was staged at Earls Court in London to celebrate Queen Victoria's Jubilee in 1887 and a further tour in 1903 was performed before Edward VII. Among 'Buffalo Bill's' cast were Annie Oakley, whose life inspired the musical *Annie Get Your Gun*, and Chief Sitting Bull, the fearsome Sioux leader who lured General Custer to his death at Little Big Horn.

An aura of romance later pervaded stories written around the many daring exploits of 'Butch' Cassidy. The less successful outlaw Sam Bass even had cowboy songs written about him, such as 'The Ballad of Sam Bass'. Ruthless killers, such as 'Billy the Kid' and Jesse James, also gained sympathy due to the folk tradition created

about them. This was mainly because both met their deaths due to treacherous acts, plus the fact that 'Billy the Kid' was kind to Mexicans. Magazines published many cartoons exaggerating their deeds.

In England, the ghosts of highwaymen reputedly haunt many inns, where centuries ago they waited to rob and terrorise lonely travellers. For example, the fifteenth-century coaching inn, now called the 'Hopcroft's Holt Hotel', still stands at what once was an eerie, lonely tree-lined crossroads at Steeple Aston, about ten miles north of Oxford. The inn claims its 'resident' ghost to be that of the notorious seventeenth-century highwayman Claude Duval, who then frequented the lonely hostelry. Towards the end of the century, his ghostly figure was held responsible for the gruesome murder of the landlord and his wife, named Spurrier. The innkeeper was discovered slain at the foot of the staircase, while his wife lay dead with a fractured skull, slumped in a nearby chair in the inglenook fireplace.

There have since been other strange happenings at the inn. Recently, in 1976, Pam Sandell, the landlord's wife, reported an odd, terrifying experience. She awoke in the darkness of her bedroom at about 1 a.m. to see the outline of a figure bent over her bed. When she overcame her initial fright, she thought it must be her husband Alan, so she called out and switched on the light. The mysterious figure vanished immediately and she saw only her husband lying asleep in bed. On another occasion, Alan Sandell and other members of his staff heard ghostly voices, together with the sound of footsteps in the unused attic. Accompanied by his dog, the landlord climbed the winding staircase but suddenly the dog refused to move forward and growled, its hair standing up on end. In 1977, a guest at the same inn became terrified when his bed began to shake violently in the middle of the night and he heard strange voices. The myth therefore remains that the ghost of Claude Duval still roams the hotel, despite the passing of three centuries.

The film industry has made a host of pictures, usually exaggerating the brave and heroic deeds of outlaws, while generally playing down the

The inn sign outside the Hopcroft's Holt Hotel at Steeple Aston, Oxfordshire. The highwayman depicted is Claude Duval whose ghost supposedly haunts the hotel. (Sonia Billett)

more sordid, brutal realities of their criminal lives. Many examples include those featuring Cartouche, Pancho Villa, Ned Kelly, Rob Roy, Dick Turpin, Jack Sheppard, Jesse James, 'Billy the Kid', 'Butch' Cassidy and the 'Sundance Kid' (1969), starring Robert Redford and Paul Newman. The English highwaywoman had also been portrayed in films such as *The Wicked Lady,* made in 1945, which starred Margaret Lockwood and James Mason, supported by Griffith Jones and Patricia Roc. A later 1983 version of the film featured Faye Dunaway and Alan Bates. There have also been innumerable film versions made of the exploits of England's legendary and probably fictional hero Robin Hood. In the early 1990s, films were still being produced, such as *Robin Hood – Prince of Thieves,* which starred Kevin Costner in the role of the outlaw.

ROBIN HOOD

Despite the tales related about his life and tragic death, no firm historical basis can be found for supposing that Robin Hood ever lived. Nevertheless, among the many conjectures is that he was born in the twelfth century, during Henry II's reign. The early stories were based in Barnsdale Woods, near Pontefract, Yorkshire, and were widely current among the peasantry. Perhaps the story-tellers created a fictitious figure to bring home the miserable plight of the poor peasants of England under the baronial system, which later culminated in the Peasants' Revolt of 1381.

Robin Hood was described as a bold, skilled archer, an expert with the quarter-staff, who outwitted the rich, especially the more pompous landowning members of the state and the monks and abbots of the church. He became the champion of the poor, just as King Arthur had earlier become the perfect knight of the upper classes in the Arthurian romances. Robin always displayed a chivalrous and sporting side to his nature and this led later to the belief that he might have been a dispossessed nobleman, rather than of peasant stock. It was suggested that he could have supported Simon de Montfort who, after his defeat at the battle of Evesham in 1265, was forced to live as an outlaw. It was also rumoured that Robin was the disinherited Earl of Huntingdon and therefore Robert Fitzooth in disguise. Another theory, based on the first recorded mention of Robin Hood, in the fourteenth-century poem *Piers Plowman*, speculated that the outlaw might have been the third member of the Randle family to become the Earl of Chester.

Early accounts of the many outlaw adventures of Robin Hood range from the late twelfth-century reign of Richard I to the early fourteenth-century period of Edward II. The first ballads, such as 'Robin Hood and the Monk', did not appear until the fourteenth century and others followed, including 'Robin Hood and the Potter' and 'Robin Hood and Guy of Gisborne'. The most important and detailed ballad, entitled 'A Lytell Geste of Roby Hode' based on the earlier versions, was probably printed in the late fifteenth century by the famous English printer Wynkyn de Worde.

The various ballads featured many of Robin Hood's companions, such as the sturdy yeoman 'Little' John, 'Will Scarlet' (William Scarlock), the miller's son Much, Allen a'Dale and George a'Green. In later ballads Friar 'Tuck' made his appearance and in a very late one of the sixteenth century, Maid Marian. The ballads made much of the money and property that Robin Hood stole and gave to the poor, but ignored the fact that he was a murderer and highwayman.

The most popular stories relating to Robin Hood centre on Sherwood Forest in Nottinghamshire rather than Yorkshire where most of the early action of the tales took place. Much of his social rebellion against authority may have stemmed from the prevailing restriction of hunting rights in the forests. The outlaw lived in the greenwood forest and led a merry band of about one hundred men who were all expert archers and had previously proved their courage and fighting ability. They mainly wore green to camouflage themselves in the forest. They poached the royal deer, and one tale told how Robin Hood, 'Little' John and 'Will Scarlet' engaged in battle with three of the king's foresters. The outlaws eventually triumphed but instead of robbing the king's gallant men, Robin gave each a 'merk', worth about thirteen shillings and four pence, to buy themselves a drink and toast his health. However, on another occasion, when greatly outnumbered, Robin Hood, with the same two companions, drew their bows and killed several of the king's men, the survivors being robbed and left tied together to an oak tree. The news swiftly spread and the Sheriff of Nottingham vowed to capture the outlaw.

The sheriff himself was robbed one day when he unsuspectingly journeyed into the forest accompanied by Robin Hood, whom he took to be a simple cattle dealer. When the outlaw blew his horn, his companions emerged from behind the trees in the forest to surround the sheriff. They then courteously entertained him to dinner, before robbing him of the gold he carried in his purse. A little later, four of Robin's men were captured when merry-making in Nottingham. They were imprisoned and sentenced to be hanged. Robin Hood's plea to the sheriff for their release fell on deaf ears and on the morning of the execution the outlaw boldly entered the town, accompanied by a hundred followers. They rescued their four companions and killed the hangman, before escaping back into the forest.

According to the ballad 'A Lytell Geste of Roby Hode', Robin later killed the Sheriff of Nottingham. In another episode, he waylaid the Bishop of Carlisle in Yorkshire as he was journeying to London, accompanied by a retinue of fifty servants. Upon being attacked, the bishop's entourage fled, although they greatly outnumbered Robin Hood's band of only ten men. The outlaws then stole 800 merks from the bishop and ridiculed him by forcing him to sing Mass. They left the unfortunate churchman tied to a tree to be released later by a passer-by.

One of the more audacious tales related that Robin Hood and some of his men entered an archery contest held in London before the king and queen, despite being wanted for murder and robbery at the time. At first, they watched the excellent shooting before wagering that they could beat the king's three best archers. The queen, impressed by Robin's charm and confidence, followed likewise with a large wager. First, Robin Hood shot his arrow and hit the centre of the target, beating his opponent easily. 'Little' John also hit the bull's-eye to defeat his adversary, as did Much the miller's son. The queen showed great delight when collecting her wager, after her successful support of the three strangers in the contest, but her husband became furious when he later learned the true identity of the disguised archers, vowing that Robin Hood would be captured and hanged. He sent a large body of soldiers into Sherwood Forest to hunt the outlaw, who was forced to go into hiding for several months in different counties. Later he returned to Nottinghamshire, to the delight of his men.

Robin Hood and his band imposed a levy on rich men travelling through their so-called forest territory and this they collected by robbing them. A tale is told of one amazing incident, when Richard I was travelling through Nottinghamshire with his entourage of noblemen. Robin, with sixty of his men, ambushed the party, killed one member for refusing to pay his levy and then relieved the others of their wealth. Robin Hood then approached the king, suggesting that as an honourable and charitable man, Richard should hand over his purse, without the need for further violence. The king had little option but to give the outlaw his gold but later vowed to see the outlaw hanged. After his escape, the king travelled to York to await the arrival of the queen. As she passed through Nottinghamshire a week later, Robin Hood and his men met her at the very spot where her husband had been robbed but gave her a warm welcome, respecting her for having previously pleaded for the lives of several captured outlaws and obtaining royal pardons for them. They dressed themselves for the occasion in their best clothes of green, trimmed with silver lace and wore smart white feathers in their caps. Then, mounted on white horses, they graciously escorted the queen's party safely to within a few miles of York before they took their leave.

Many years later, in the final days of his legendary life, Robin Hood retired to a monastery in Yorkshire after he became very ill. Although he had successfully eluded capture and the threat of hanging for twenty years, he suffered a miserable death at the hands of his cousin, the wicked prioress of Kirklees. The prioress and her secret lover, Sir Roger of Doncaster, plotted to end the outlaw's life. She treacherously bled him to death when supposedly pretending to relieve his malady. Thus ended the legend of Robin Hood.

BIBLIOGRAPHY

Adams, James T. and Coleman, R. V. (eds), *Dictionary of American History*, Charles Scribner's Sons, New York, 1951.

Ash, Russell, *Discovering Highwaymen,* Shire Publications Ltd., Buckinghamshire, 1994.

Bagust, Harold, *London Through the Ages*, Thornhill Press, 1982.

Barker, F. and Silvester-Carr, D., *The Black Plaque Guide to London*, Constable, 1987.

Black, Jeremy, *Eighteenth Century Europe 1700–1789*, Macmillan, 1990.

Bland, James, *The Book of Executions*, Warner, 1993.

Chambers, R. (ed.), *The Book of Days*, Vol 1, W. and R. Chambers, 1864.

Chisholm, Alec H. (ed.), *The Australian Encyclopaedia*, Angus and Robertson, 1958.

Clark, Manning, *History of Australia*, Chatto and Windus, 1993.

— (ed.), *Oxford History of the American West*, Oxford University Press, 1994.

— (ed.), *The American Destiny (The Age of the West)*, Orbis, 1986.

— (ed.), *The World Book Encyclopaedia*, various Vols. World Book Corp., Chicago, 1995.

— (ed.), *The World of Adventure*, Vol 1, Cassell, 1889.

Evans, H., *Hero on a Stolen Horse*, Muller, 1977.

Farrugia, Jean and Gammons, Tony, *Carrying British Mail*, National Postal Museum, London, 1980.

Fielding, Henry and Saintsbury, George (ed.), *The History of the Life of the late Mr Jonathan Wild the Great*, Vol 10 of *The Works of Henry Fielding,* J. M. Dent, 1893.

Griffiths, Arthur, *The Chronicles of Newgate*, Bracken Books, 1987.

Haining, Peter, *The English Highwayman*, Robert Hale, 1991.

Holt, J. C., *Robin Hood*, Thames and Hudson, 1982.

Johnson, Nichola, *Eighteenth Century London*, Museum of London, 1991.

Jones, Colin, *The Cambridge Illustrated History of France*, Cambridge University Press, 1994.

Kamen, Henry, *The Iron Century. Social Change in Europe 1550–1660*, Weidenfeld and Nicolson, 1971.

Lamar, Howard R. (ed.), *The Reader's Encyclopaedia of the American West*, Harper and Row, 1977.

Maguire, Morgan, Reiner (eds) *The Oxford Handbook of Criminology*, Clarendon Press, Oxford, 1994.

Markham, George, *Guns of the Wild West*, Arms and Armour Press, 1991.

McKnight, S., *Stage Coach and Highwayman*, Wayland Publishers, 1973.

McLynn, Frank, *Crime and Punishment in Eighteenth Century England*, Oxford University Press, 1991.

Milford, Humphrey (ed.), *Dictionary of American Biography*, Oxford University Press, 1929.

Munck, Thomas, *Seventeenth Century Europe 1598–1700*, Macmillan, 1990.

Newark, P. and May, R., *The Old West*, Bison Books Corporation, 1984.

Rayner, J. L. and Crook, G. T. (eds), *The Complete Newgate Calendar*, 4 vols. Private Print for the Navarre Society, London, 1926.

Rienits, Rex and Thea, *A Pictorial History of Australia*, Hamlyn, 1969.

Rosa, Joseph G., *Guns of the American West*, Arms and Armour Press, 1985.

Rose, Lionel, *Crime and Punishment*, B. T. Batsford, 1977.

Rudé, George, *Hanoverian London 1714–1808*, Secker and Warburg, 1971.

Smith, Captain Alexander and Haywood, Arthur (ed), *A Complete History of the Highwaymen*, Routledge, 1933.

Treasure, Geoffrey, *The Making of Modern Europe, 1648–1780*, Methuen, 1985.

Utley, Robert M., *Billy the Kid: A Short and Violent Life*, I. B. Tauris, 1990.

Wilde, W. H., Hooton, J. and Andrews, B., *The Oxford Companion to Australian Literature*, Oxford University Press, 1986.

Younger, R. M., *Australia and the Australians*, Rigby, Adelaide, 1970.

INDEX

NOTICE
—
£100 REWARD
WILL BE PAID
TO THE PERSON
WHO CAPTURES
DICK TURPIN